Frances Eales
Steve Oakes

speakout

Starter
Students' Book

with ActiveBook

CONTENTS

LESSON	GRAMMAR/FUNCTION	VOCABULARY	PRONUNCIATION	READING
UNIT 1 HELLO page 7 ▣ Video podcast | Where are you from?				
1.1 Where are you from? page 8	be: I/you	countries	word stress in country names	
1.2 Arrivals page 10	be: he/she/it	jobs	pronunciation of sentences with is	read an article about arrivals at an airport
1.3 How do you spell … ? page 12	giving personal information	the alphabet	intonation in Wh- questions	
1.4 Around The World page 14		places and adjectives		
UNIT 2 PEOPLE page 17 ▣ Video Podcast | Who is in your family?				
2.1 Family photos page 18	be: you/we/they	family	pronunciation of you're, we're, they're	
2.2 A family business page 20	possessive adjectives	numbers 11–100	pronunciation of numbers	read about family businesses
2.3 Let's have a break page 22	making suggestions	feelings	intonation in answers	
2.4 Royal Wedding page 24				
REVIEW 1 page 27	be: all forms; possessive adjectives		sounds: /æ/ and /ə/	read messages at a festival
UNIT 3 THINGS page 29 ▣ Video podcast | What are your favourite things?				
3.1 What's this? page 30	this/that/these/those	objects	/s/ /z/ /ɪz/ in plurals	
3.2 Whose shoes? page 32	possessive 's	clothes and colours		read an article about famous objects
3.3 A coffee, please page 34	ordering in a café	food and drink	intonation in or questions	
3.4 The Market page 36		objects in a market		
UNIT 4 LIFE page 39 ▣ Video podcast | What do you do for fun?				
4.1 What's different? page 40	present simple: I/you/we/they	verb phrases	intonation in yes/no questions	
4.2 Double lives page 42	present simple: he/she/it	days; time phrases	present simple verb endings: /s/, /z/ and /ɪz/	read an article about avatars
4.3 What time is it? page 44	telling the time	events		
4.4 Rivers page 46				
REVIEW 2 page 49	present simple		sounds: /s/ and /z/	read a description of people's jobs
UNIT 5 ROUTINES page 51 ▣ Video Podcast | What do you usually do at the weekend?				
5.1 Bad habits page 52	present simple questions: he/she/it	daily routines	linking: does he/she/it	
5.2 Superman and supermodel page 54	adverbs of frequency	food	numbers of syllables; stress in adverbs of frequency	read an article about what a sportsman and a model eat
5.3 When does it open? page 56	asking for information	hotel services	stress in a conversation; intonation to show interest	
5.4 Doctor Who page 58				

LANGUAGE BANK page 118   PHOTO BANK page 138

CONTENTS

LISTENING/DVD	SPEAKING	WRITING
listen to personal introductions	introduce yourself	learn to use capital letters
	ask questions about people and places	
listen to conversations at reception	learn to check spelling; exchange personal information	
BBC Around The World: watch an extract from a documentary about people around the world	talk about yourself and your country	write a personal introduction
listen to someone talk about family photos	talk about photos of family and friends	learn to use contractions
	check information about people	
listen to people making suggestions	learn to respond to suggestions; make suggestions about where to go	
BBC The Royal Wedding: William and Catherine: watch an extract from a documentary about a royal wedding	talk about five people in your life	write a description of people in your life
listen to conversations at a festival	ask personal information; talk about your family	
listen to conversations in offices	ask for the names of things in English	
	talk about clothes	link sentences with *and* and *but*
listen to conversations in a café	learn to say prices; do a role-play in a café	
BBC Francesco's Mediterranean Voyage: watch an extract from a travel programme about a market	do a role-play in a market	write a description of a market
listen to people talk about life in the USA.	talk about things you have in common	link sentences with *and* and *because*; write a blog about your life
	find differences in pictures	
listen to conversations about times	tell the time; learn to check times; ask people to come to events	
BBC Human Planet: Rivers: watch a documentary about rivers	talk about your favourite season	write a forum reply about your favourite season
listen to a conversation about a woman's favourites	talk about your favourite thing; guess the jobs	
listen to conversations about people's bad habits	talk about habits that drive people crazy	
	answer a questionnaire about your daily routines	link sentences with *first*, *then*, *after that*, *finally*
enquiries in a hotel	learn to show interest; do a role-play at a tourist information desk	
BBC Doctor Who: watch a drama about a time-travelling doctor	talk about food to take to a desert island	write a forum entry about food to take to a desert island

COMMUNICATION BANK page 148   AUDIO SCRIPTS page 154

CONTENTS

LESSON	GRAMMAR/FUNCTION	VOCABULARY	PRONUNCIATION	READING
UNIT 6 JOURNEYS page 61 ▣ Video podcast | How do you get to school or work?				
6.1 No trains page 62	*there is/are*	places	stress in sentences with *there is/are*	
6.2 Getting there page 64	*a/an, some, a lot of, not any*	transport	stress in sentences with *a/an, some, a lot of, not any*	read a text about transport facts
6.3 Single or return? page 66	buying a ticket	travel	learn to check numbers	
6.4 Rush Hour page 68		transport		
REVIEW 3 page 71	present simple: *he/she/it* questions; *there is/are*; *a/an, some, a lot of, not any*		sounds: /ð/ and /θ/	read a website problem page
UNIT 7 PAST page 73 ▣ Video podcast | Where were you on your last birthday?				
7.1 Where were you? page 74	past simple: *was/were*	dates	weak forms of *was/were*	
7.2 Record breakers page 76	past simple: regular verbs	actions	past simple regular verbs with /t/, /d/ and /ɪd/	read an article about amazing records
7.3 How was it? page 78	giving opinions	adjectives	intonation for positive/negative feelings	
7.4 The Chilean Miners page 80				
UNIT 8 PLACES page 83 ▣ Video podcast | Where did you go on holiday last year?				
8.1 Nice place to meet page 84	past simple: irregular verbs	prepositions of place (1)		read about how people met their friends
8.2 Good and bad page 86	past simple: questions	holiday activities	linking in *did you*	
8.3 Where's the fruit? page 88	giving directions	prepositions of place (2)		
8.4 Guided Tour page 90		holidays		
REVIEW 4 page 93	past simple: *was/were*; regular and irregular verbs		sounds: /ʌ/ and /ʊ/	read a newspaper report and police statements about a crime
UNIT 9 SHOPPING page 95 ▣ Video podcast | Do you like shopping?				
9.1 The right gift page 96	*like, love, hate + -ing*	activities		read about gift-giving around the world
9.2 A waste of money page 98	object pronouns	money	pronouns in connected speech	
9.3 What would you like? page 100	making requests	shopping departments	intonation in polite offers or requests	
9.4 Days That Shook The World page 102		music players		
UNIT 10 PLANS page 105 ▣ Video podcast | What did you want to be?				
10.1 A new job page 106	*can/can't*	collocations	strong and weak forms of *can/can't*	read adverts for interesting jobs
10.2 Time for a change page 108	*be going to*	life changes	pronunciation of *going to*	
10.3 Hello and goodbye page 110	starting and ending conversations	saying goodbye	stressed words in phrases	
10.4 Miranda page 112		problems		
REVIEW 5 page 115	*like, love, hate + -ing*; object pronouns; *can/can't*; *be going to*		sounds: /ɑː/ and /ɜː/	do a questionnaire about what you can do in English
LANGUAGE BANK page 118			**PHOTO BANK** page 138	

CONTENTS

LISTENING/DVD	SPEAKING	WRITING
conversations at a station	ask about places; find differences between two pictures	learn to start and end an email
	ask and answer questions about transport; compare cities' transport	
listen to someone buy a bus ticket	learn to check numbers; do a role-play at a train or bus station	
BBC **Visions Of India: Rush Hour:** watch an extract from a documentary about India	talk about travel in your country	write a travel forum entry
listen to problems in different situations	role-play problems in different situations	
listen to conversations about New Year 2000	ask where people were in the past	improve your punctuation
	talk about what you/others did in the past	
listen to people giving opinions	give your opinion; learn to show feelings	
BBC **The Chilean Miners' Rescue:** watch an extract from a documentary about the Chilean miners' rescue.	do a history quiz	write a history quiz
	talk about first meetings	
listen to a radio programme about holidays	talk about a good holiday	link sentences with *so* and *because*
listen to people ask directions in a supermarket	do a role-play in a supermarket; learn to use examples	
BBC **Little Britain Abroad:** watch an extract from a comedy about tourists in Spain	tell a bad holiday story	write a story about a bad holiday
listen to people talk about the crime	find differences in two students' stories	
	talk about likes and dislikes; choose an activity gift for a student	
listen to a radio programme about shopping mistakes	talk about shopping	write captions for your photos
listen to someone shopping	learn to use hesitation phrases; choose a birthday present	
BBC **Days That Shook The World: Into The 21st Century:** watch an extract from a documentary about the arrival of the MP3 player	describe a possession	write about a favourite possession
listen to job interviews	talk about ability; do a quiz to find the best job for you	
listen to street interviews about people's goals	discuss your plans and goals	learn to check your work
listen to people start and end conversations	learn to respond naturally; do a role-play at a party	
BBC **Miranda:** watch an extract from a comedy about a woman who wants to change her life	talk about learning something new	write a magazine interview about learning something new
listen to students talk about learning English	discuss ways of improving your English; play the Speakout Game	

COMMUNICATION BANK page 148   AUDIO SCRIPTS page 154

NUMBERS 1–10

1A Match the words in the box with the numbers.

| ~~zero~~ nine three one seven ten four two |
| eight five six |

0	_zero_	4	_____	8	_____
1	_____	5	_____	9	_____
2	_____	6	_____	10	_____
3	_____	7	_____		

B ▶ **L.1 Listen and check. Then listen and repeat.**

C ▶ **L.2 Listen and write the numbers.**

D Work in pairs and take turns. Student A: say a number. Student B: say the next number.

1 *A: five*   *B: six*
2 *B: zero*   *A: one*

INTERNATIONAL ENGLISH

2A Match the words in the box with photos 1–6.

| DVD *1* phone hotel football bus chocolate |

B ▶ **L.3 Listen and check. Then listen and repeat.**

C Work in pairs. Write five more international words.

▷ page 138 **PHOTOBANK**

CLASSROOM LANGUAGE

3A ▶ **L.4 Listen and underline the correct word.**

Conversation 1
A: OK, Antonio. *What's*/ *Is* 'libro' in English?
B: Sorry, I *not*/ *don't* know.
A: It's 'book'.
B: Can you *write*/ *say* it, please?
A: Yes …

Conversation 2
A: OK. Open your books, please.
B: Sorry, I *no*/ *don't* understand.
A: Open, like this.
B: Which *page*/ *number*?
A: Page eight.
B: Can you *repeat*/ *write* that, please?
A: Yes, page eight.
B: Thank you.

B Work in pairs and take turns. Practise the conversations.

▷ page 138 **PHOTOBANK**

speakout TIP

Start a phrasebook. Write useful phrases, e.g. *Hello, Hi, Good morning, Good afternoon, Good evening, Good night.*

UNIT 1

SPEAKING
- ❯ Introduce yourself
- ❯ Ask questions about people
- ❯ Give personal information
- ❯ Check spelling
- ❯ Speak about yourself and your country

LISTENING
- ❯ Listen to people say *hello*
- ❯ Listen to people give personal information
- ❯ Watch a BBC programme about people around the world

READING
- ❯ Read descriptions of people arriving at an airport

WRITING
- ❯ Learn to use capital letters
- ❯ Write a personal introduction

BBC CONTENT
- ▯ Video podcast: Where are you from?
- ◉ DVD: Around the World

UNIT **1**

hello

▶ **Where are you from?** p8   ▶ **Arrivals** p10   ▶ **How do you spell … ?** p12   ▶ **Around The World** p14

| ▶ **GRAMMAR** \| be: I/you | ▶ **VOCABULARY** \| countries | ▶ **HOW TO** \| introduce yourself |

A

B

C

LISTENING

1A ▶ 1.1 Listen and match conversations 1–4 with photos A–D.

1 _B_   2 ____   3 ____   4 ____

B Listen again and match the person with the country and city.

1	Carmen	Ireland Australia Spain the USA	Dublin Cork Sydney Melbourne Barcelona Madrid New York San Francisco
2	Cindy		
3	Tom		
4	Katie		

GRAMMAR be: I/you

2A Complete the tables with 'm and are.

I	'm	Carmen. from Spain

Where	_____	you	from?
	_____	you	from Sydney?

Yes,	I	am.	
No,		_____ not.	

B ▶ 1.2 Listen and underline the stressed words.
I'm Carmen.

C Listen again and repeat the sentences.
▷ page 118 **LANGUAGEBANK**

D

PRACTICE

3A Complete the conversations with 'm or are.
Conversation 1
A: Hello, I ¹_'m_ Janet.
B: Hi, I ²_____ Paul. Nice to meet you.
A: Nice to meet you, too. Where ³_____ you from?
B: I ⁴_____ from South Africa.
A: Oh, where in South Africa?
B: From Cape Town.
Conversation 2
A: Hello, I ¹_____ Kasia.
B: Hi, I ²_____ Peter.
A: Nice to meet you.
B: Nice to meet you, too. Where ³_____ you from?
A: I ⁴_____ from Poland.
B: ⁵_____ you from Warsaw?
A: No, I'm not. I'm from Gdansk.

B ▶ 1.3 Listen and check.

C Work in pairs and practise the conversations.

D Work in pairs and talk about your name, country and town/city.
A: Hello, I'm …
B: Hi, I'm …

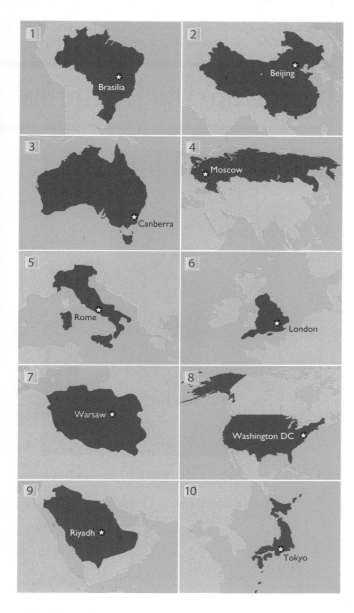

▮▮➡ page 139 **PHOTOBANK**

VOCABULARY countries

4A Match the countries in the box with pictures 1–10.

> Brazil *1* Japan Russia Poland China England
> Australia Italy the USA Saudi Arabia

B ▶1.4 Listen and check.

C Listen again and underline the stress. Then listen and repeat.
Brazil

D Work in pairs and take turns. Student A: say a number. Student B: say the country.
A: *four*   **B:** *Russia*

speakout TIP

Write new words in your notebook and underline the stress, e.g. *Japan*, *Italy*.

WRITING capital letters

5A Underline the capital letters in sentences a)–f).
a) I'm Karin.
b) I'm Ali Mansour.
c) Are you from Saudi Arabia?
d) No, I'm from England, from London.
e) Are you a student?
f) Yes, I am.

B Match rules 1–5 with sentences a–f above.

> Rules:
> Use capital letters for:
> 1 the name of a person   *a), b)*
> 2 a country
> 3 a city
> 4 I
> 5 The first word in a sentence.

C Find and correct the mistakes with capitals in the chat messages below.

1 hi, i'm jeanette, and i'm a teacher in france. *Hi,*

2 hi, i'm makiko. i'm from japan. are you from paris?

3 no, i'm from lyon. are you from tokyo?

4 yes, i am. i'm a student.

6A Work in pairs. Write a chat message to your partner.
Hi, I'm …

B Swap messages. Answer the message.
A: *Hi, I'm …*
B: *Hi, I'm …*

SPEAKING

7A Write a country and a city from the country.
England – Manchester

B Work in groups and take turns. Guess the cities.
A: *Where are you from?*
B: *I'm from England.*
A: *Oh, are you from London?*
B: *No, I'm not.*
A: *Are you from … ?*

VOCABULARY jobs

1A Write the jobs in the box under pictures 1–8.

> teacher   actor   engineer   doctor   taxi driver
> businessman/businesswoman   singer   waiter

1

2

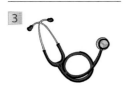
3

4

5

6

7

8

B ▶ 1.5 Listen and check. Then listen and repeat.

2A Look at the conversation. Underline the correct alternative in the rules.

A: Are you a teacher?

B: No, I'm a student, an English student. Are you an actor?

A: No, I'm a singer, an Italian singer.

> **Rules:**
> 1 Use *a/an* with words starting with vowels (*a, e, i, o, u*)
> 2 Use *a/an* with words starting with consonants (*b, c, d ...*)

B Work in pairs and take turns. Student A: say a job. Student B: say *a* or *an*.

A: doctor   *B: a doctor*

C Work with other students. Student A: mime a job. Other students: guess the job.

B: Are you an engineer?

A: No, I'm not.

C: Are you a doctor?

A: Yes, I am.

▸ page 139 **PHOTOBANK**

Welcome to Heathrow

Ajay Kumar is a computer engineer from Delhi in India. He's in England for an International Conference. 'It isn't my first time in England, but it's my first time in London.'

READING

3A Work in pairs. Look at the photos of people at Heathrow Airport, London. Who is a tourist?

B Read the texts and check your answer.

C Complete the table with the correct information.

name	Ajay			
job		actor/ waiter		
where from?			Mexico	
first time in London?				no

Rosa Pérez López is from Mexico. She's a doctor from Acapulco. She's in London on holiday. 'I'm very happy. It's my first time in England.'

Nicolas Dupont is from France. 'I'm an actor in Paris, but now I'm a waiter here in a café in London. London's a good city for actors.'

Gong Yue is a student from China. 'I'm from Shanghai, but now I'm a business student at the University of London.' 'Is it a good university?' 'Yes, it is!'

GRAMMAR   be: he/she/it

4A Underline the verb *be* in the sentences.

1 Ajay Kumar <u>is</u> a computer engineer.
2 She's a doctor from Acapulco.
3 It isn't my first time in England.
4 Is it a good university? Yes, it is.

B Complete the tables.

He She It	is 's	from France.
	is not _____	

	he/she/it	from India? a doctor? your first time here?
Yes,	he/she/it	is.
No,		_____.

Where	_____	he	from?

C ▶ 1.6 Listen and write sentences 1–5. Then listen and repeat.

⟹ page 118 **LANGUAGEBANK**

PRACTICE

5A Add *'s* (*is*) in ten places.

Ellie Turner's from Montreal, Canada. She a teacher at McGill. It a big university in Montreal. She in London for a conference.

Yong-Joon from Korea. He a taxi driver in Seoul, the capital. He in London on holiday. He happy to be here.

Pat a businesswoman from Auckland, New Zealand. She in London on business.

B Write the questions.

1 Ellie / Canada?
   Is Ellie from Canada?
2 she / doctor?
3 McGill University / London?
4 Yong-Joon / Japan?
5 he / London / on holiday?
6 Auckland / New Zealand?

C Match answers a)–f) to questions 1–6 above.

a) No, it isn't. *3*   d) No, he isn't.
b) Yes, he is.   e) Yes, it is.
c) Yes, she is.   f) No, she isn't.

D Cover the answers above. Work in pairs and ask and answer questions 1–6.

SPEAKING

6 Work in pairs and take turns. Student A: turn to page 148. Student B: turn to page 152.

▶ **FUNCTION** | giving personal information   ▶ **VOCABULARY** | the alphabet   ▶ **LEARN TO** | check spelling

VOCABULARY the alphabet

1A ▶1.7 Listen and repeat the letters.

Aa Bb Cc
Dd Ee Ff
Gg Hh Ii
Jj Kk Ll
Mm Nn Oo
Pp Qq Rr
Ss Tt Uu
Vv Ww Xx
Yy Zz

B Complete 1–7 with letters from the box. Each group has the same vowel sound.

H Y T E W J M S

1 A *H* __ K
2 B C D __ G P __ V
3 F L __ N __ X
4 I __
5 O
6 Q U __
7 R

C ▶1.8 Listen and check. Then listen and repeat.

D Work in pairs. Student A: turn to page 148. Student B: turn to page 152.

A

FUNCTION giving personal information

2A ▶1.9 Listen and match conversations 1–3 with photos A–C.
1 ___   2 ___   3 ___

B Listen again and complete the information.

	First name	Family name	Room number
1		*Taylor*	
2			
3			

3A Complete the form with the words in the box.

~~First name~~ Email address Nationality Family name Phone

Riverside Gym

MEMBERSHIP FORM

First name:	Stefanie
:	Young
:	American
number:	0532 419
:	stef@yahoo.com

B

C

B Underline the correct alternative. Check your answers in audio script 1.9 on page 154.

1 A: What's/are your first name?

   B: Stefanie.

2 A: How do you spell/say that?

   B: S-t-e-f-a-n-i-e.

3 A: What's your phone number?

   B: It's ow/oh five three two, four one nine.

4 A: What's your email address?

   B: It's stef at/it yahoo point/dot com.

C ▶ 1.10 Listen and tick the correct intonation. Then listen and repeat.

a) What's your email address?

b) What's your email address?

▶ page 118 **LANGUAGEBANK**

4A Write a phone number and an email address.

B Work in pairs and take turns. Ask questions and write the answers.
A: What's your phone number?
B: It's 382 7492.

LEARN TO check spelling

5A ▶ 1.11 Listen to the conversation and underline the stressed letters.
A: And your first name?
B: It's Frances.
A: F-r-a-n-c ... is it i-s?
B: No, e. E as in England. F-r-a-n-c-e-s.

speakout TIP

Some names of letters are difficult, for example Y, J and G, I and E. Write words to help you remember, e.g. Y as in 'yes', J as in 'Japan'. Do this for G, I and E now.

B Work in pairs and correct the spelling.

1 Obdul – Abdul
   A: Is it O-b-d-u-l?   **B:** *No, A. A as in Australia. A-b-d-u-l.*
2 Stevin – Steven
3 Cinthia – Cynthia
4 Suzan – Susan
5 Geanette – Jeanette
6 Eves – Yves

SPEAKING

6 Work in groups and take turns. Ask and answer questions to complete the table.

	Student 1	Student 2	Student 3
First name			
Family name			
Nationality			
Phone number			
Email address			

Canada

Santiago, Chile

Malaysia

Kuala Lumpur, Malaysia

Helsinki, Finland

Oman

DVD PREVIEW

1A Work in pairs. Find the words in the box in the photos.

city	countryside	sea	beach
mountain	river	village	building

B Work in pairs and take turns. Say an adjective from the box below and a word from the box above.

old	new	big	small	beautiful
cold	hot			

A: *an old city*   B: *an old building*   A: *an old …*

2 Read the programme information and underline the countries.

BBC Around The World

In this programme, people from around the world answer the questions: *Who are you? Where are you from? What's your job?* We speak to Kustaa in Finland, Mizna in Oman, Pablo in Chile, Aisha in Malaysia and Eric in Canada.

▶ DVD VIEW

3A Watch the DVD and number the places in the order you see them.

a) British Columbia, Canada ___
b) Santiago, Chile   _1_
c) Helsinki, Finland   ___
d) Kuala Lumpur, Malaysia ___
e) Muscat, Oman   ___

B Work in pairs. Which things from Exercise 1A are in the places?

Chile   *building, mountain*

C Watch the DVD again to check your answers.

D Work in pairs and underline the correct alternative. Then watch the DVD again to check your answers.

1 Santiago, Chile is *old/old and new*.
2 The mountains in Chile are *hot/cold*.
3 Eric is a *waiter/driver* on a train.
4 Mizna is a *teacher/student* at university.
5 She is from a *city/village*.
6 In Finland, the countryside is good for *winter/summer* sport.
7 Kuala Lumpur is a(n) *old/new* city.
8 Aisha is a(n) *shop/office* assistant.

speakout you and your country

4A ▶ 1.12 **Listen and answer the questions for Kaitlin.**

Name: _Kaitlin_

1 Where are you from?   _____
2 Is your city big or small?   _____
3 Is your city old or new?   _____
4 What's your job?   _____
5 Where's your job?   _____
6 Is English important for you?_____
7 Is the countryside beautiful? _____

B **Listen again and tick the key phrases you hear.**

keyphrases

Hello or 'dia duit' from Ireland.

I'm/My name's …

I'm a/an (teacher/engineer) in …

Dublin/Cannes is a (city/a town/a village) in …

It's/It isn't very (big/beautiful/hot/small/old/new).

The countryside (in Ireland) is beautiful.

I (really) love it (here).

5A **Prepare to talk for thirty seconds. Write your answers to the questions in Exercise 4A. Use the key phrases to help.**

B **Work in pairs and take turns. Student A: give your talk. Student B: listen and ask Student A two questions.**

writeback a personal introduction

6A **Read the personal introduction for a class blog. Tick the information in the introduction.**

a) name ✓   e) city
b) nationality   f) country
c) email address   g) 'Hello' and 'Goodbye'.
d) job   h) languages

aboutme.com   Rita Peterson's blogspot

Hello, or 'hallo' in German. I'm Rita Petersen and I'm from Germany. I'm a businesswoman with Volkswagen. I speak German and English in my job.

I'm from Berlin, the capital city of Germany. Berlin is a city with a mix of old and new buildings. The countryside in Germany is beautiful, with mountains and rivers.

5 comments   posted by Rita

B **Write a personal introduction. Use the introduction above to help. Write 50–70 words.**

BE: I/YOU

1A Complete the conversation with the words in the box.

~~Are~~ 'm I am in you not six

A: [1] _Are_ you from Rome?
B: No, I [2]_____ not.
A: Are [3]_____ from Seoul?
B: Yes, I [4]_____.
A: Are you [5]_____ Tokyo now?
B: No, I'm [6]_____.
A: Are you number [7]_____?
B: Yes, [8]_____ am.

B Work in pairs and take turns. Student A: choose a sentence from 1–6 below. Student B: ask questions and guess the sentence.

1 I'm from Rome. I'm in London now.
2 I'm from Madrid. I'm in Cork now.
3 I'm from Seoul. I'm in Tokyo now.
4 I'm from Rome. I'm in Cork now.
5 I'm from Madrid. I'm in Tokyo now.
6 I'm from Seoul. I'm in London now.

B: Are you from Madrid?
A: Yes, I am.
B: Are you in Cork?
A: No, I'm not.
B: Number 5!

COUNTRIES

2A Work in pairs. Write the countries.

1 Torino _Italy_
2 Calcutta I_____
3 St. Petersburg R_____
4 Mecca S_____ A_____
5 Xian C_____
6 Osaka J_____

B Write five countries and a city in each country.
China – Beijing

C Work in pairs and take turns. Student A: say a city. Student B: say the country.
A: Beijing
B: China

JOBS

3A Add the vowels to the jobs.

1 w__ __ t__r
2 t__x__ dr__v__r
3 __ng__n__ __r
4 d__ct__r
5 __ct__r
6 t__ __ch__r
7 s__ng__r
8 b__s__n__ssw__m__n

B Work in groups. Student A: choose your job. Other students: guess the job.
A: Are you a nurse?
B: No, I'm not.
C: Are you a doctor?
B: Yes, I am.

BE: HE/SHE/IT

4A Find and correct the wrong information in the sentences below.

1 Madrid is in Portugal.
   No, it isn't. It's in Spain.
2 Vladimir Putin's from Canada.
3 The Eiffel Tower's in Argentina.
4 Jackie Chan's from South Africa.
5 Maria Sharapova's from Poland.
6 Tokyo's in Italy.
7 Queen Elizabeth is from Spain.
8 The Taj Mahal's in Mexico.
9 Barack Obama's from Scotland.
10 Kylie Minogue's from China.

B Work in pairs. Write three false sentences – one about a man, one about a woman, and one about a place.

C Work with other students and take turns. Student A: say a sentence. Other students: say the correct information.
A: Cate Blanchett is from Canada.
B: No, she isn't. She's from Australia.

THE ALPHABET

5A Correct the spelling.

1 fone _phone_
2 televison _____
3 camra _____
4 univercity _____
5 resterant _____
6 emial _____
7 futbal _____
8 choklat _____
9 infomashion _____
10 intenet _____

B Work in pairs and take turns. Ask and answer about the spelling.
A: How do you spell 'phone'?
B: p-h-o-n-e.
A: Right.

GIVING PERSONAL INFORMATION

6A Look at the information and write questions for 1–5.

Dr [1]Hakan [2]Osman

Bilkent University, Ankara, [3]Turkey.
[4]Phone: 039 387 4425
[5]Email: Osman@mail.bilkent.edu.tr

1 What's your first name?

B Change three things in 1–5 above.
Phone: 034 387 4425

C Work in pairs and take turns. Student A: ask questions 1–5. Student B: answer the questions. Student A: find the three changes.

UNIT 2

SPEAKING
❯ Talk about photos of family and friends
❯ Check information about people
❯ Suggest things to do
❯ Talk about five people in your life

LISTENING
❯ Listen to someone talk about photos
❯ Watch a BBC programme about a royal wedding

READING
❯ Read about family businesses

WRITING
❯ Use contractions
❯ Describe five people in your life

BBC CONTENT
🖥 Video podcast: Who is in your family?
◉ DVD: Royal Wedding

UNIT **2**

people

▶ **Family photos** p18   ▶ **A family business** p20   ▶ **Let's have a break** p22   ▶ **Royal Wedding** p24

▶ **GRAMMAR** | *be: you/we/they*   ▶ **VOCABULARY** | family   ▶ **HOW TO** | talk about your family

Looker

You aren't signed in   Sign in   Help

Home   The Tour   Sign up   Explore ▼ Upload

Search

VOCABULARY family

1A Match people 1–6 with photos A–F.

1 husband and wife   4 mother and daughter
2 brothers and sister   5 parents and children
3 father and son   6 parents and daughter

B ▶ 2.1 **Listen and underline four words with the sound /ʌ/. Then listen and repeat.**

husband

C Work in pairs. Complete the table with the family words from Exercise 1A.

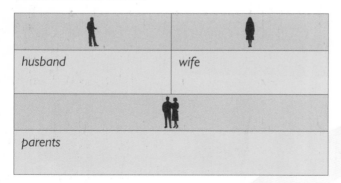

husband	wife
parents	

D Work in pairs and take turns. Student A: say a photo A–F. Student B: say who it is.

A: Photo E   B: mother and daughter

LISTENING

2A ▶ 2.2 **Listen to the conversations. Which four of the photos (A–F) are they talking about?**

1 ____   2 ____   3 ____   4 ____

B Listen again. Match the names in the box with sentences 1–6.

~~Margit~~   Tim   Erika (x2)   Johnny   Lewis   Flori

1 She's Hungarian. *Margit and ...*
2 He's a businessman.
3 She's married to an Englishman.
4 She's seven.
5 He's at university.
6 He's a musician.

GRAMMAR *be: you/we/they*

3A Underline the verb *be* in the sentences.

1 A: Where are you?
B: We're at home.

2 A: Are they students?
B: Yes. Johnny's at university.

3 A: You aren't English?
B: No, we aren't English.

B Complete the tables below with the words in the box.

~~'re~~ Are aren't are (x2)

You We They	are 're	from Spain. students. English.
You We They	are not _____	teachers. from Poland.
_____	you/we/they	in the right classroom?
Yes,	you/we/they	_____.
No,		aren't.
Where	_____	you from?

C 2.3 Listen to the pronunciation of *you're, we're, they're*. Then listen and repeat.

D 2.4 Listen and write the sentences in your notebook. Then listen and repeat.

page 120 LANGUAGEBANK

PRACTICE

4A Underline the correct alternative.

A: This is a photo of Dan.
B: [1]*Is he/Are you* brothers?
A: No, [2]*I'm not/we aren't*. [3]*He's/We're* good friends.
B: And this photo? [4]*Are they/Is she* your sisters?
A: No, they [5]*isn't/aren't*. This is my wife, Maria, with Tina. Tina and Maria are sisters. The photo is in Peru.
B: Are [6]*they/she* from Peru?
A: No, they [7]*not/aren't*. [8]*They're/She's* from Uruguay.
B: [9]*Is/Are* your wife a teacher?
A: Yes. She and Tina [10]*is/are* teachers.

B Work in pairs and practise the conversation.

WRITING contractions

5A Look at the example. Complete the contractions for sentences 2–4.

1 They are my parents. *They're my parents*
2 She is my daughter.
3 We are not sisters.
4 Tom is my brother.

B Underline the correct alternative to complete the rules.

Rules:
1 *Use/Don't use* contractions in spoken English.
2 *Use/Don't use* contractions in text messages and emails to friends.

C Rewrite the text messages using eight contractions.

1
Hi, Marianna. ~~I am~~ *I'm* at the airport, but your brother is not here. What is his mobile number? It is not in my phone. Tom

2
Hi, Tom. I am sorry, I don't know. We are in an English class now.

3
Hi, Marianna. It is OK. Luca is here now. See you soon. T

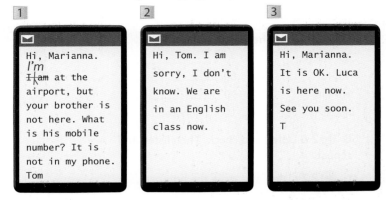

D Work in pairs and take turns. Read out the text messages with the contractions.

speakout TIP

Prepositions (*at, in, to, from*) are small but important. Underline the prepositions in the sentences.
I'm at the airport. We're in a lesson. Are they from Peru? She's married to an Englishman. It's the capital of Italy.

SPEAKING

6A *EITHER* Use two photos of your family or friends and complete the notes below. *OR* Work in pairs. Student A: look at the photos on page 148. Student B: look at the photos on page 152.

Photo 1

Name:
Family or friend:
Nationality:
Job:
Where is he or she now?

Photo 2

Name:
Family or friend:
Nationality:
Job:
Where is he or she now?

B Work with other students. Cover your notes and talk about the photos.

This is my brother, Juan. He's South African. He's an office worker in Cape Town.

VOCABULARY numbers 11–100

11 12 **13** 14 **15** 16 **17** 18 **19** 20

1A Write the numbers next to the words.

eleven	_11_	fifteen	____
nineteen	____	fourteen	____
twenty	____	sixteen	____
thirteen	____	eighteen	____
twelve	____	seventeen	____

B ▶ 2.5 Listen and repeat the numbers in order.

C Work in pairs and take turns. Student A: write a number. Student B: say the number.

2A Complete the numbers.

30	thirty	70	_____
40	forty	80	_____
50	fifty	90	_____
60	sixty	100	a hundred

B ▶ 2.6 Listen and check. Then listen and repeat.

C ▶ 2.7 Listen and write the numbers.
1 67

3A Write the names and ages of four friends or people in your family.
Eloise 53   Andreas 28

B Work in pairs and take turns. Student A: tell Student B about the people. Student B: write down the names and ages.
A: Eloise is my mother.
B: How old is she?
A: She's fifty-three.
B: How do you spell Eloise?

READING

4A Work in pairs and look at the photos. What is the relationship between the people (e.g. husband and wife)?

B Read the text and check your ideas.

C Read the texts again and complete the information.

	Business	Where?	Good things
1	restaurant		small, friendly
2			
3			

Morelli's Restaurant is in downtown New York. The managers are Italians Alfonso Morelli and his sister Enrica. Her husband, Frederico, is the cook. 'Our restaurant is five years old. It's a real family business. It's small and friendly and the food is fantastic.'

Star Supermarket is in the centre of Edinburgh, Scotland, and its doors are open 24/7*. Sixty-year-old manager, Alex, is from Jamaica. His wife, Dana, and daughters, Sakina and Mia, and their husbands are the shop assistants. 'We're a family business,' says Dana, 'and we're open 24/7 because people shop 24/7.'

*24/7: twenty-four hours a day, seven days a week

Hotel de Coin is a ten-room hotel in Paris. It's a small family business. The manager, Oskar, is Estonian and his wife, Brigitte, is French.' It's a family business,' says Oskar. 'My wife is the receptionist and our sons are the cooks. The hotel is only fifteen minutes from the city centre. On holiday or on business, it's the perfect place for your stay.'

GRAMMAR possessive adjectives

5A Complete the sentences with *my, your, his, her, its, our, their*. Then check your answers in the texts in Exercise 4A.

1 The managers are Italians Alfonso Morelli and __his__ sister Enrica. _____ husband, Frederico, is the cook.

2 Star Supermarket is in the centre of Edinburgh, Scotland, and _____ doors are open 24/7.

3 His wife, Dana, and daughters, Sakina and Mia, and _____ husbands are the shop assistants.

4 'It's a family business,' says Oskar. '_____ wife is the receptionist and _____ sons are the cooks.' He says, 'It's the perfect place for _____ stay.'

B Complete the table.

subject pronoun	possessive adjective	subject pronoun	possessive adjective
I	my	it	_____
you	_____		our
_____	his	they	_____
she	_____		

page 120 **LANGUAGEBANK**

PRACTICE

6A Underline the correct alternative.

1 The boss is a woman – *his/her* name is Mani.
2 *His/Her* husband Kasem is the receptionist.
3 Kasem isn't happy in *his/my* job.
4 *Our/Their* business is in a very beautiful place.
5 *Your/Its* name is 'Tasanee'.
6 Mani says, '*Our/Their* rooms are very good'.
7 Kasem says, 'Yes, but *my/our* job isn't good!'

B Work in pairs. What is the business in Exercise 6A?

7 Complete the sentences with the words in the box. Do **not** use one of the words.

~~my~~ your his her its our their

Mama's salsa – from mother of three, Lucia Covas Garcia

'The salsa recipe is from ¹ _my_ mother, and ² _____ name is *Mama's Salsa*. It's a hundred years old' says Lucia. ³ _____ husband Manolo and ⁴ _____ son Pablo are all in the family business. 'Pablo and ⁵ _____ wife, Sonja are the cooks and ⁶ _____ salsa is on sale all over South America.'

SPEAKING

8A Work in pairs. Student A: turn to page 148. Student B: look at the information below. Make questions to find the missing information.

How old is Gerhardt Becker?
What's his … ?

Gerhardt Becker, _____ (age), and Julia Becker, 35, are husband and wife. Gerhardt is _____ (nationality) and Julia is from Canada. Their business is in _____ (city), and they're taxi drivers. Their company name is _____ (name) and their special taxi-bus is good for families and big groups.

Jon and Liz _____ (family name) are brother and sister, and their Moroccan restaurant, *Rocco*, is in _____ (country). They're not from Morocco, they're from England, but their restaurant is very good for Moroccan food.

B Work in pairs and take turns. Ask and answer the questions.

▶ **FUNCTION** | making suggestions   ▶ **VOCABULARY** | feelings   ▶ **LEARN TO** | respond to suggestions

VOCABULARY feelings

1A Match the adjectives in the box with pictures A–F.

hot D   cold   hungry   thirsty   tired   bored

B Work in pairs and take turns. Student A: ask about a problem and point to a picture. Student B: say the problem.
A: What's the problem?
B: I'm tired.

▶ page 140 **PHOTOBANK**

A

FUNCTION making suggestions

2A ▶ 2.8 Listen and match conversations 1–3 with photos A–C.

1 ____   2 ____   3 ____

B Listen again. Are the sentences true (T) or false (F)?
1a) They're in school.
 b) Café Lugo is a Spanish cafe.
2a) It isn't their first meeting.
 b) His first name's Lee.
3a) They're tired and hot. *T*
 b) They're hungry.

C Correct the false sentences.

3A Which verbs in the box are in the photos?

eat   have a coffee/cola   have a break   sit down   go   stop

B Listen again and complete the conversations with a verb from Exercise 3A. Do <u>not</u> use one of the verbs.
1 A: I'm hungry.
  B: Yeah, me, too. Let's _____ *eat* _____.
2 A: Nice to meet you, too.
  B: Let's _____. Coffee?
  A: Yes, please.
3 A: Let's _____.
  B: Good idea. I'm tired.
4 A: Let's _____.
  B: Yeah, OK. Let's _____.

C Complete the rule.

Rule:
Use _____ + verb to make a suggestion.

D ▶ 2.9 Listen and underline the stressed words in Exercise 3B. Then listen and repeat.
Let's e̲at.

▶ page 120 **LANGUAGEBANK**

4A Complete the conversations with the words in the box.

'm problem Me too break 's a Let

1 A: I ^{1} __'m__ bored.
  B: Me, ^{2}_____.
  A: ^{3}_____'s stop now.
  B: Good idea.

2 A: What's the ^{4}_____?
  B: I'm cold.
  A: Me, too. Let ^{5}_____ go inside.
  B: OK.
  A: OK, let's have a ^{6}_____ for fifteen minutes.

3 B: I'm thirsty.
  A: ^{7}_____, too.
  B: Let's have ^{8}_____ coffee.

B Work in pairs and practise the conversations.

 respond to suggestions

5A ▶ 2.10 Listen to the answers. Are they interested (+) or not interested (−)? Tick + or − .

1 ⊕ ✓ ⊖   3 ⊕ ⊖
2 ⊕ ⊖   4 ⊕ ⊖

 speakout TIP

Use intonation to show you are interested or happy.

Great!

B Work in pairs and take turns. Student A: say *Great/OK/ Good idea.* Student B: point to + or − .

⊕ ⊖

SPEAKING

6A Work in pairs and complete the conversation.

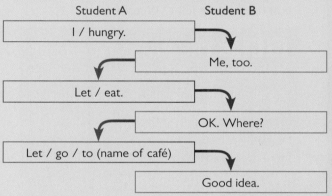

Student A	Student B
I / hungry.	
	Me, too.
Let / eat.	
	OK. Where?
Let / go / to (name of café)	
	Good idea.

B Work in pairs and practise the conversation.

7 Work with other students. Start your conversation with the adjectives. Make suggestions for places to go.

tired hungry hot thirsty cold bored

A: I'm tired.
B: Me, too.
A: Let's go and have a coffee.
B: Good idea. Where?
A: Let's go to …

DVD PREVIEW

1A Work in pairs and look at the photos. What is the relationship to William and Kate?

A: *Prince Harry is his brother.*

B: *Yes, and I think Prince Charles is his ...*

Prince William

Kate Middleton

Queen Elizabeth and Prince Philip

Prince Charles

Prince Harry

Pippa Middleton

David and Victoria Beckham

Elton John

B Read the programme information. Who is at the royal wedding? Where is it?

BBC The Royal Wedding: William and Catherine

Thousands of people are in the streets of London and billions of people around the world are by their TVs, all for the royal wedding of Prince William and Kate Middleton. The BBC programme *Royal Wedding* is the story of their big day. Their families and friends are all at Westminster Abbey for the wedding.

▶ DVD VIEW

2A Watch the DVD and number the people in Exercise 1A in the order you see them.

David and Victoria Beckham 1

B Correct one word in each sentence.

1 Today is the ~~birthday~~ *wedding* of Prince William and Kate Middleton.

2 Victoria and David Beckham, friends of Prince William, are hungry.

3 Kate and her brother go to Westminster Abbey.

4 Her sister, Pippa Middleton arrives with daughters of friends and family.

5 The big moment ... and a woman with the ring.

6 The end of a big holiday for Kate and William.

C Watch the DVD again to check your answers.

speakout five people in your life

3A ▶ 2.11 Listen to Jo talk about five people in her life. Match the names with people 1–5.

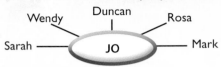

Wendy   Duncan   Rosa

Sarah — JO — Mark

1 a person in her family   *Duncan*
2 a student in her class
3 a good friend
4 her teacher
5 a person at her work

B Listen again and tick the key phrases you hear.

keyphrases

OK, five people in my life. The first is ... (name)

Duncan's (my brother/a very good friend).

We're on the phone a lot.

I'm (a shop assistant/an office worker) and Mark's my manager.

(She/He's) very nice, very friendly.

Wendy is a (worker in my office/student in my class).

We're in a Spanish class together.

We're good friends.

C Write the names of five people in your life.

D Work in pairs and take turns. Talk about your five people.

writeback a description

5A Read the information and answer the questions.

1 Who is in her family?
2 Who isn't a friend?
3 Who is her best friend?

Five people in my life

My name is Claudia. I'm twenty-nine and I'm an IT worker. Here are five people in my life:

Betsy: She's my best friend from university. She's twenty-eight and she's in Munich, Germany. She's an actress.

Dennis: He's my brother. He's twenty-six, and he's a very good friend. He's a teacher in Japan.

Ali: She's my mother and she's my friend. We're on the phone a lot.

Edith: She's a friend from work. She's a happy person and a very good friend.

Pasqualo: He isn't a friend, but he's a nice person. He's from Italy. He's a waiter at a restaurant in my city.

B Write about five people in your life.

FAMILY

1A Look at the diagram. Write the names of the people.

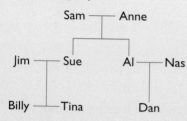

1 My father is Sam and my sister is Sue. *Al*
2 My daughter is Tina and my wife is Sue.
3 My mother is Sue and my sister is Tina.
4 My parents are Sam and Anne and my brother is Al.
5 My son is Dan and my husband is Al.
6 My children are Sue and Al and my husband is Sam.

B Write three more sentences about the people in the diagram.
1 My brother is ...

C Work in pairs and take turns.
Student A: read out a sentence.
Student B: say the name.

BE: YOU/WE/THEY

2A Complete the conversation with the words in the box.

are (x4)   is (x2)   they (x3)
we   're

1 A: Who __are__ they?
2 B: _____'re my friends Ali and Hesna.
3 A: Where _____ _____ from?
4 B: _____'_____ from Syria.
5 A: _____ you friends from school?
6 B: No, _____'re friends from university.
7 A: _____ they married?
8 B: Ali _____n't married. Hesna _____ married to my brother.

B Write the names of two of your friends.

C Work in pairs and take turns. Ask and answer questions about the friends.

NUMBERS 11–100

3A Write the numbers in words.
1 twenty-one + (plus) nine =
   thirty
2 ninety-nine – (minus) eleven =
   _____
3 eighty-three + fourteen =
   _____
4 thirty-two – five =
   _____
5 fifty-six + twelve =
   _____

B Complete the questions with a number.
1 What's 62 – _____?
2 What's 15 + _____?
3 What's 81 – _____?
4 What's 19 + _____?

C Work in pairs and take turns. Ask and answer the questions.

POSSESSIVE ADJECTIVES

4A Find and correct the mistakes in the sentences.
1 I'm Chinese and I'm name's Jun.
2 You're in Room 108 and Mr Watts is you're teacher.
3 He's John. He's family name's Wayford.
4 She's name's Vera and she's a singer.
5 We're students and we're class is Room Ten.
6 They're names are Ahmed and Ali and they're from Egypt.

B Complete the sentences about yourself and other students. Write five true sentences and one false sentence.
1 I'm _____ and my _____.
2 You're _____ and your _____.
3 _____'s from _____ and his _____.
4 _____'s from _____ and her _____.
5 We're _____ and our _____.
6 Their _____ and they're _____.

I'm Veronika and my family name's Keta.

C Work in pairs and take turns.
Student A: read your sentences.
Student B: which sentence is false?

FEELINGS

5A Add the vowels to complete the feelings.
1 h_o_t
2 h__ngry
3 t_r__d
4 c__ld
5 th__rsty
6 b_r__d

B Work in pairs and take turns.
Student A: close your book.
Student B: mime a feeling.
Student A: say the feeling.

MAKING SUGGESTIONS

6A Put the words in the correct order to complete the conversation.
A: go / Let's / now
B: tired / I'm / No, / Let's / down / sit.
A: a / let's / and / have / stop / OK, / break
B: Are / thirsty / you?
A: Yes / am / I
B: to / go / Let's / café / a
A: idea / Good

B Work in pairs. Write one key word from each sentence.
go
tired
stop
thirsty

C Work in pairs and practise the conversation. Use the key words to help.

READING AND GRAMMAR

1A Work in pairs and look at the pictures. Where are they?

B Read the messages. Write the names next to the letters of the pictures.

A _____ B _Bruno_ C _____ D _____
E _____

1

> Hi, everybody! I'm Sandra and I'm from Scotland.
> I'm here with my brother, Neil. He's also Scottish,
> of course. We're office workers in Edinburgh. Neil
> is a big music fan. It's my first time, and I'm very
> happy to be here. We're in the Festival Hotel in
> room 217 – please come and say hello!

2

> Binny is a singer from Jaipur, India. She's
> twenty-four years old and is at festivals all over
> the world. Her music is a mix of traditional
> Indian and modern rock. Her concert is tonight at
> 8p.m. Please come and see her sing!

3

> **LOST**
> Fifi and Bruno, my two dogs. Fifi is black and
> she's one year old. Bruno is white and he's four.
> They're very friendly. If Fifi and Bruno are with
> you, text me (Jasmine) on 443 908 9442.

C Read the messages again. What are the numbers?
Write *age*, *room*, or *phone* and the name.

4 _____ _age, Bruno_
217 _____
4439089442 _____
24 _____
1 _____

D What music festivals are in your country? Are they good?

2A Complete the questions with words from the box. Do not use one of the words.

> are (x 2)   they   her   his   is (x 2)   it   how

1 _Are_ Sandra and Neil from Ireland?
2 _____ Neil a singer?
3 Is Sandra _____ sister?
4 Where _____ Binny from?
5 When is _____ concert?
6 _____ Fifi and Bruno cats?
7 Are _____ friendly?
8 _____ old is Bruno?

B Work in pairs and take turns to ask and answer the questions.

A: Are Sandra and Neil from Ireland?
B: No, they aren't. They're from Scotland.

3 Complete the messages with the correct form of *be*.

> I' **1** _m_ here with a group of students from St
> Petersburg, and we' **2** _____ at the festival for the first
> time. My room **3** _____ in the student hotel. The hotel
> **4** _____(not) very nice, but the hotel workers **5** _____ all
> very friendly. **6** _____ you here alone? Don't be alone –
> come and see us. Let's have a party!

> ✉
> Arturo, **7** _____ you here? Where are you? Jeff and I
> **8** _____ at the HJ Hotel in room 102. Please come and
> see us! Robin

LISTENING

Morelli   Fatimah   Churchill

Cho   Takahashi   Gonzales

4A Work in pairs and look at the names of people at the festival. What nationality are the people?

B ▶ R1.1 Listen and check.

C Listen again. Who talks about food (F), drink (D), music (M)?

1 ___   2 ___   3 ___

SPEAKING

5 Work in pairs. Student A: turn to page 153. Student B: look at the table below. Ask questions to complete the information.

First name	¹Frank	²Fatimah	³Neil and Sandra
Family name		Hassan	
Nationality	Korean		Scottish
Age		23	
Job	teacher		office workers
Email address	33chocho@yahoo.com		NeilMac42@hotmail.com SandyMac@phonex.co.uk

B: Number one is Frank. What's his family name?
A: Cho.
B: How do you spell it?
A: C-h-o. What's his nationality?

6A Write the names of three people in your family. Write their ages, jobs, relationship to you (*brother, mother*, etc) and where they are now.

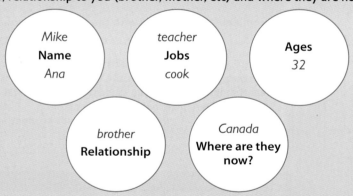

Mike **Name** *Ana*

teacher **Jobs** *cook*

Ages *32*

brother **Relationship**

Canada **Where are they now?**

B Work in pairs and take turns. Look at your partner's information. Ask and answer about each person.
A: Is Mike your brother?
B: Yes, he is.
A: Is he a teacher?
B: No, he isn't. He's a cook.
A: Is he in Canada?

SOUNDS: /æ/ AND /ə/

7A ▶ R1.2 Listen to the sounds and the words. Then listen and repeat.

/æ/	/ə/
taxi	teacher

B ▶ R1.3 Listen and put the words in the box in the correct group. Then listen and repeat.

~~doctor~~   ~~actor~~   England   nationality
computer   understand   happy
daughter

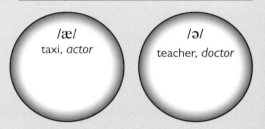

/æ/	/ə/
taxi, *actor*	teacher, *doctor*

8A Work in groups. Complete the words and circle the sound in each word.

	/ə/
a country	Br@zil
son and daughter	ch_____
a number	se_____
www	in_____
TV	te_____
a country	In_____

	/æ/
it's for photos	c@mera
mother, father, son and daughter	fa_____
woman in a film	ac_____
money place	ba_____
big letters	ca_____
a job	ma_____

B Work with other students and compare your answers.

UNIT 3

SPEAKING
> Ask about objects
> Talk about possessions
> Order food and drink
> Buy things in a market

LISTENING
> Listen to conversations in an office
> Listen to people in a café
> Watch a BBC programme about a famous market

READING
> Read descriptions of famous possessions

WRITING
> Use linkers: *and, but*
> Write about a market

BBC content
> Video podcast: What are your favourite things?
> DVD: Francesco's Mediterranean Voyage

things

▶ **GRAMMAR** | *this/that/these/those*   ▶ **VOCABULARY** | objects   ▶ **HOW TO** | ask the names for things

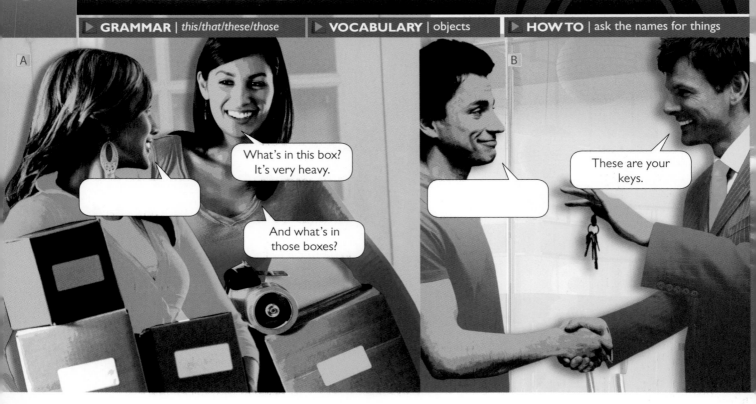

VOCABULARY objects

1A Work in pairs and look at photos A–D. Which objects in the box are <u>not</u> in the photos?

> computer   printer   desk   keys   clocks   lamp
> business cards   boxes   picture   chair

B Which words in the box are singular and which are plural? Write *S* or *P*.

C ▶ 3.1 Look at the pronunciation of the plural words. Then listen and repeat.
/s/ clock<u>s</u>
/z/ card<u>s</u> key<u>s</u>
/ɪz/ box<u>es</u>

▸ page 140 **PHOTOBANK**

LISTENING

2A ▶ 3.2 Listen and match conversations 1–4 with photos A–D.

1 _____   2 _____   3 _____   4 _____

B Listen again. Who is <u>not</u> happy? Circle two names.

> Sam   Mr Stanford (Bill)   Anne   Jill   Mr Fletcher
> Janet   Denise

C Work in pairs and look at photos A–D. Complete the conversations with 1–4 below. Check your answers in audio script 3.2 on page 155.

1 And is that your new computer?
2 My keys?
3 It's my new printer.
4 Nice.

GRAMMAR this/that/these/those

3A Circle *this, that, these, those* in the conversations in photos A–D.

B Write *this, that, these, those* under pictures 1–4.

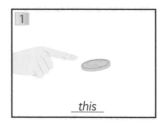
this

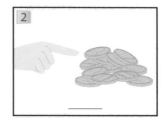
_____

_____

_____

C Complete the rule with *is* or *are*.

> Rule:
> I Use *this/that* + _____.
> I Use *these/those* + _____.

D ▶ 3.3 Listen and tick the word you hear. Then listen and repeat.

1 a) this   b) these
2 a) this   b) these
3 a) these   b) those
4 a) these   b) those

▸ page 122 **LANGUAGEBANK**

PRACTICE

4A Miki is a new student in a language school. Complete the conversations with *this, that, these* or *those*.

A: Miki, ¹ _this_ is the students' room and ² _____ are my friends over there.

B: Where are they from?

A: They're from Italy and Brazil. Hi, everyone. ³ _____ is Miki, from Japan.

B: Hello.

A: OK, Miki. Here's our classroom and ⁴ _____ is our teacher, Mrs King. Mrs King!

C: Yes. Who's ⁵ _____ ? Oh hello, Sylvie. And you're the new student, yes?

B: Yes, I'm Miki. Hello.

C: Hello, Miki. Welcome to the class. ⁶ _____ is your coursebook.

B: Thank you.

C: And have one of ⁷ _____ dictionaries here.

B: Thanks.

C: Please sit down. ⁸ _____ desk is free, over there by the window.

B Work in groups and practise the conversations.

⟨ speakout TIP

For your phrasebook: introduce people with *This is* + name: *This is my sister, Tina. This is Dr Meyer.*
Mr = man; *Mrs* = married woman; *Miss* = single woman;
Ms = married or single woman; *Dr* = Doctor

SPEAKING

5A Work in pairs. Choose three objects in the classroom and three objects from your bag.

B Write the English words for the objects. Look in a dictionary or ask your teacher.

C Work in groups and take turns. Point to your objects and ask questions.

A: What are those in English?

B: They're windows. What's this in English?

C: I don't know.

D: It's a purse.

▶ **GRAMMAR** | possessive 's   ▶ **VOCABULARY** | clothes and colours   ▶ **HOW TO** | talk about clothes

The Museum of Memorabilia: Top Six

Are you interested in famous people? What about famous objects? A glove, a dress, a guitar? The Museum of Memorabilia* is a museum of famous people's things, but what are the Top Six? Read the list and find out:

1 Elvis Presley's guitar. Presley is The King of Rock and Roll, or simply The King. This is his guitar from the film *Love Me Tender*.

2 Usain Bolt's gold running shoes. Bolt is Jamaican and is a three-time Olympic gold medallist.

3 Venus Williams's tennis racquet. Williams and her sister, Serena, both from the USA, are the winners of over 45 major tennis competitions.

4 Daniel Radcliffe's glasses. They aren't really Daniel's but they're Harry Potter's glasses from the films. The English actor is famous as Harry Potter, but is also famous for his acting in theatre.

5 Michael Jackson's glove. Jackson is still called 'The King of Pop' and this is the most famous glove in the world.

6 Marilyn Monroe's white dress. Monroe fans all know this dress – it's from the 1955 film *The Seven Year Itch*.

*memorabilia = objects from famous people, places, films, sports, etc.

READING

1A Work in pairs and look at photos 1–6 above. What's in the museum?

B Work in pairs. Match the objects in the photos with the famous people on page 33.

C Read the text and check your ideas.

D Read the text again and find:
- two names of films
- two singers
- two clothes
- two sports people
- two nationalities

2A Work in pairs and think about music, films and sport. Write the names of three objects from famous people.

B Work in groups and choose one object for the museum.

GRAMMAR possessive 's

3A Add 's in the correct place in each sentence. Use the text to help.
1 These are Daniel Radcliffe's glasses.
2 These are Usain Bolt gold running shoes.
3 This is Michael Jackson glove.
4 This is Venus Williams tennis racquet.

B ▶ 3.4 Listen and check. Then listen and repeat.

C Complete the rule.

Rule: Use a name + ___ for the possessive.

▶ page 122 **LANGUAGEBANK**

PRACTICE

4A Complete the questions.
1 these / Nico / books?
   Are these Nico's books?
2 that / Yasmin / chair?
3 those / the teacher / shoes?
4 this / Carolyn / phone?
5 these / James / pens?

B Change questions 1–5 to make questions about students and things in your classroom.
1 Are these Nico's books?   *Is this Emir's book?*

C Work in pairs and take turns. Ask and answer the questions.

A Elvis Presley
B Marilyn Monroe
C Michael Jackson
E Usain Bolt
D Venus Williams
F Daniel Radcliffe

VOCABULARY clothes and colours

5A Write the names of clothes 1–6 under pictures A–F below.

1 T-shirt 3 hat 5 jacket
2 sweater 4 shirt 6 trousers

B Work in pairs. Match the clothes with the famous people in the photos above.

A: I think these are Michael Jackson's trousers.
B: No, I think they're Elvis Presley's.

C ▶ 3.5 Listen and check your ideas.

D Match the colours in the box with the clothes in pictures A–F below. Then listen again and check.

| black   blue   brown   red   white   yellow |

▶ page 141 **PHOTOBANK**

A

B

C

D

E

F

6A Write four sentences about people's clothes in your class. Write two true sentences and two false sentences.
Nina's shoes are red.

B Work in pairs and take turns. Student A: read a sentence. Student B: say if it's true or false.

WRITING linkers *and, but*

7A Complete the sentences with *and* or *but*.

1 Argentinean football shirts are blue _____ white.
2 Marilyn Monroe's famous dress is white _____ her famous hat is white, too.
3 Serena Williams's favourite colour is blue _____ her tennis dress is white.

B Complete the sentences with *and* (x2) or *but* (x2).

1 These are Gisele Bündchen's sunglasses *and* hat. Her name is German she's Brazilian.
2 This is basketball player Luol Deng's red shirt. Deng isn't from Britain he's in the British basketball team he's in an American team: the Chicago Bulls.

C Complete the sentences with *and* and *but*.

1 This / be / actress Penelope Cruz / hat. Cruz / be / from Spain / she / be / in American films.
2 This / be / football player Miroslav Klose / shirt. Klose / be / from Poland / his / nationality / be / German / he / be / in / the German national team.

SPEAKING

8 Work in pairs. Student A: turn to page 149. Student B: turn to page 151.

| ▶ **FUNCTION** | ordering in a café | ▶ **VOCABULARY** | food and drink | ▶ **LEARN TO** | say prices |

VOCABULARY food and drink

1A Look at the photo. What is it? Where is it?

B Read the information and find the country names.

> The very first American-style Hard Rock Café (now forty years old) is in the centre of London, England. There are Hard Rock Cafés and Hotels in fifty-two countries around the world: from Hong Kong in China to Caracas in Venezuela and Prague in the Czech Republic. The cafés are full of rock and roll memorabilia: guitars, photos and even a Cadillac from the 1950s.

C Work in pairs and answer the questions.

1 What is in every Hard Rock Café? Do you know a Hard Rock Café?

2 What cafés are good in your town/city?

2A Match phrases 1–6 with pictures A–F.

1 A sandwich and a coffee   A

2 A tea and a cake   B

3 A mineral water and a sandwich   C

4 A cola and a cake   D

5 A tea and a mineral water   E

6 A coffee and a cola   F

B Work in pairs and check your answers.

C Work in pairs and cover the words in 1–6 above. Take turns to order the food and drink.

A: Can I help you?

B: A sandwich and a coffee, please.

A: OK, here you are.

FUNCTION ordering in a café

3A ▶ 3.6 Listen to the conversations and correct the customers' orders.

1 1 white coffee with sugar

2 2 espresso coffees and 1 cappuccino

3 1 egg sandwich (white bread), 1 chocolate cake, 1 cola

4 1 sparkling mineral water, 1 sandwich

B Who says the sentences? Write C (customer) or W (waiter).

a) How much is that? C

b) Anything else?

c) Still or sparkling?

d) Can I have a mineral water, please?

e) No, thank you.

f) That's two euros.

g) Sparkling, please.

C ▶ 3.7 Number sentences a)–g) in order. Then listen and check.

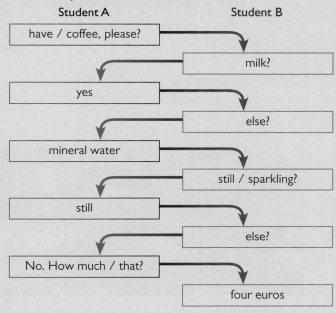

5A Complete the conversation.

Student A · Student B

Student A	Student B
have / coffee, please?	
	milk?
yes	
	else?
mineral water	
	still / sparkling?
still	
	else?
No. How much / that?	
	four euros

B Work in pairs and take turns. Practise the conversation.

➠ page 122 **LANGUAGEBANK**

LEARN TO say prices

6A ▶ 3.9 Listen and number the prices in order.

3.00	2.50	10	1.50 *1*	5.20	12.75

B Listen again and repeat.

speakout TIP

Say prices with the name (e.g. euros) or with no name:
3.99 = three euros ninety-nine OR three ninety-nine.

C Write four prices in your country's money.

D Work in pairs and take turns. Student A: read the prices. Student B: write the prices.

SPEAKING

7 Work in pairs. Student A: turn to page 148. Student B: turn to page 152.

4A Complete the table.

_____ I have	a	mineral water, please?
	two	coffees, _____?
Still		sparkling?
Espresso	_____	cappuccino?
		Sparkling, please.
		Espresso, please.

B ▶ 3.8 Listen and tick the intonation you hear. Then listen and repeat.

1 Still or sparkling?   2 Still or sparkling?

C Work in pairs and take turns. Ask and answer using the words in the box.

| Coffee / tea?   Espresso / cappuccino? |
| Still / sparkling? |

A: *Coffee or tea?*   **B:** *Tea, please.*

DVD PREVIEW

1A Match objects 1–6 with pictures A–F.

1	spices *E*	4	jewellery
2	clothes	5	pottery
3	carpets	6	leather wallets and bags

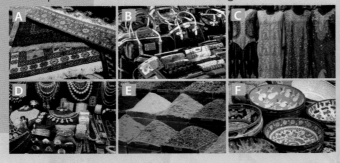

B Which objects in Exercise 1A are in markets in your town or city?

2 Read the programme information. Where is Francesco? What is his new job?

BBC Francesco's Mediterranean Voyage

Francesco da Mosto is an Italian TV presenter. In this programme Francesco is in Istanbul, Turkey, at the Grand Bazaar – Istanbul's famous market. His new 'job' is a carpet seller but he says 'I don't know anything about carpets!' His friend and teacher, Harkan, helps him. Is Francesco a good salesman?

▶ DVD VIEW

3A Watch the DVD. Which objects in Exercise 1A are in the market? Tick the objects.

B Watch the DVD again and underline the word you hear in the sentences.

1 My *first / second* day in Istanbul.
2 There are four *hundred / thousand* shops here.
3 I'm here to *study / learn*.
4 This is *new / nice*. This looks old but it is not old.
5 This is a *free / real* art. Like Turkish Picasso.
6 It's *not good / a nightmare*!
7 A: Three hundred dollars.
   B: *Eight / Nine* hundred.
8 Americans are good. They are *friendly / beautiful*.
9 It's his first *carpet / sale*.
10 We will give you a special *discount / price*, five hundred dollars.

C Work in pairs and answer the questions.
1 Is Francesco a good salesman?
2 Is Harkan (the Turkish man) a good salesman?

speakout in a market

4A ▶ 3.10 Listen to the conversation. Are the sentences true (T) or false (F)? Correct the false sentences.

1 The lamps are from Morocco. *F*
   They're from Turkey.
2 The seller's first price is 215.
3 The woman's first price is 50.
4 The final price is 150.

B Listen again and tick the key phrases you hear.

keyphrases

Excuse me.
Where is (this/that) (lamp/carpet) from?
Where are (these/those) (lamps/carpets) from?
Can I have a look?
This one?
No, that one.
How much (is it/are they?)
That's expensive.
For you, a special (discount/price.)

C Work in pairs and take turns. Student A: you are the customer. Choose an item from Exercise 1A. Student B: you are the seller. Choose a price. Role-play the situation.

writeback a description

5A Read the description of a market and answer the questions.

1 What's the name of the market?
2 Where is it?
3 Is it open every day?
4 What is it good for?

Covent Garden market is in the centre of London. It's open every day and it's good for beautiful jewellery, clothes and pictures. It's also good for small shops and cafés. It's a famous tourist attraction for visitors to London and there are people from all over the world. I'm not a tourist, I'm from London, but for me Covent Garden market is a good place to stop and have a break.

B Write about a market in your town/city or another town/city. Answer the questions in Exercise 5A.

OBJECTS

1 Add the vowels to complete the objects.

1 ke̲y̲
2 c__mp__t__r
3 d__sk
4 ch__ __r
5 print__r
6 b__s__n__ss c__rd
7 cl__ck
8 b__x
9 l__mp
10 p__ct__r__

THIS/THAT/THESE/THOSE

2A Complete the conversation with *this, that, these* or *those*.

Jan: Maria, ¹ *this* is my husband, Carlos. Carlos, ²_____ is my friend from school, Maria.

Carlos: Hello, Maria. Nice to meet you.

Maria: Nice to meet you, too. Are ³_____ your children?

Carlos: Yes, ⁴_____ is my daughter, Ana, and ⁵_____ is my son, Paolo.

Maria: Hi.

Carlos: Say 'Hi' to Maria.

Ana and

Paolo: Hi.

Carlos: Is ⁶_____ your car over there?

Maria: Yes, it is. And ⁷_____ are my children in the car. Come and say 'Hi'.

B Work in groups and practise the conversation.

C Work in pairs. Write a new name, nationality and job for your partner.

Naomi, Greek, hairdresser

D Work in groups. Introduce your partner.

A: Yuko, this is Naomi. Naomi, this is Yuko.

B: Hi …

POSSESSIVE 'S

3A Complete the captions with a name from the box.

S̶h̶a̶k̶e̶s̶p̶e̶a̶r̶e̶	Mozart
Michael Jordan	Galileo
Bill Gates	Picasso

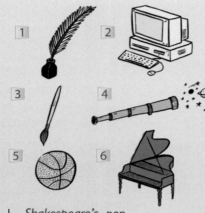
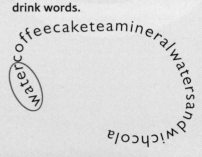

1 _Shakespeare's_ pen
2 _____ computer
3 _____ brush
4 _____ telescope
5 _____ basketball
6 _____ piano

B Work in pairs and take turns. Student A: choose a student's possession. Say *It's …* and the name of the person. Student B: Ask three questions to find the object.

A: It's Radu's.
B: Is it Radu's pen?
A: No, it isn't.
B: Is it … ?

CLOTHES AND COLOURS

4A Put the letters in the correct order to make four clothes and four colours. The first letter is underlined.

1 s̲erds   5 t̲ajeck
2 k̲labc   6 l̲oywel
3 l̲beu   7 re̲tsours
4 t̲hirs   8 no̲rbw

B Write three more clothes and three colours.

C Work in pairs and take turns. Student A: say a word. Student B: spell it.

A: hat   B: h-a-t

FOOD AND DRINK

5 Find and circle seven food and drink words.

watercoffeecaketeamineralwatersandwichcola

ORDERING IN A CAFÉ

6A Complete the conversation.

A: ¹help / you? *Can I help you?*
B: ²egg sandwich
A: ³White / brown?
B: ⁴White
A: ⁵else?
B: ⁶mineral water
A: ⁷Still / sparkling?
B: ⁸Sparkling. How much / that?
A: ⁹$5.90
B: ¹⁰here / are

B Work in pairs and practise the conversation. Then cover your answers and practise it again.

7A Complete the pairs with your ideas.

1 coffee / ___tea___
2 cappuccino / _____
3 still / _____
4 euros / _____

B Work in groups. Student A: say one of your words and *or*. The other students: complete the question. Pay attention to the intonation.

A: Coffee   or   … ?
B: Coffee   or   tea?

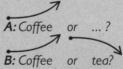

UNIT 4

SPEAKING
> Find things in common
> Find differences in pictures
> Tell the time
> Talk about your favourite season

LISTENING
> Listen to people talk about life in the USA
> Listen to people tell the time
> Watch a BBC programme about life on a river

READING
> Read about people and their avatars

WRITING
> Use linkers: *and, because*
> Write about your favourite season

BBC content
> Video podcast: What do you do for fun?
> DVD: Rivers

UNIT
4

life

What's different? p40

Double lives p42

What time is it? p44

Rivers p46

VOCABULARY verb phrases

1A Complete the word webs with the verbs in the box.

~~like~~   study   work   do   have   go   live   drive

coffee — I _like_ — clothes (football)

a phone — 2 _____ — a cola (a brother)

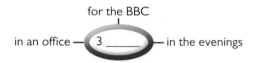

in an office — 3 _____ — in the evenings (for the BBC)

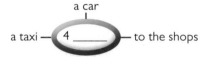

a taxi — 4 _____ — to the shops (a car)

at university — 5 _____ — ten hours a week (English)

with my parents — 6 _____ — in a flat (in a house)

to Spain — 7 _____ — to room ten (to a café)

Exercise 3A — 8 _____ — sport (your homework)

B Work in pairs. Which phrases from Exercise 1A are in the photos?

C Work in pairs and take turns. Student A: say a sentence about yourself. Student B: say if it's true for you.

A: I like coffee.
B: Me, too. (✓) I work in an office.
A: I don't. (✗)

❞ speakout TIP

It's good to learn verb phrases (*work in an office*), not just verbs (*work*). Write verb phrases in your notebook.

⟫ page 142 **PHOTOBANK**

LISTENING

2A Read the programme information. Are the people from the USA?

11a.m. – The USA Today

People from different countries speak about their life in the USA. Is life in the USA the same or different from their countries?

B ▶ 4.1 Listen and number the topics in the order people talk about them. One topic is <u>not</u> in the listening.

friends   students   American football   houses *1*   cars

C Listen again and underline the correct alternative.

1 'In the USA, people live in *houses/flats*.'
2 'Students have jobs in the *mornings/evenings*.'
3 'People *drive/walk* two hundred metres to the shops.'
4 'My American friends like *the same/different* things.'

GRAMMAR present simple: *I/you/we/they*

3A Underline the verbs in the sentences.

1 We <u>live</u> in flats.
2 They work in the evenings.
3 You like the same things.
4 I don't drive to the shops.

B Complete the table.

+	I You	like	sport.
–	We They	_____ live	in a house.

▶ page 124 **LANGUAGEBANK**

PRACTICE

4A Complete the sentences with a verb in the positive or negative.

1 I _____ *live* _____ with a friend. (+)
2 I _____ two sisters. (+)
3 I _____ a camera. (–)
4 I _____ English five hours a week. (+)
5 I _____ in an office. (–)

B Tick the sentences above that are true for you. Change the sentences that aren't true.

1 I don't live with a friend. I live with my parents.

WRITING *and, because*

5A Read the blog entry. Which things are the same in your life?

My two cities

I'm from Toronto, Canada, but I work in Osaka, Japan, six months a year. I like life in Japan, but it's very different.
In Toronto, I live in a big house and I drive to the shops because they're five kilometres from my house. In Osaka, I live in a small flat and I walk to work because I don't have a car. I'm often tired because we work six days a week.

B Complete the sentences with *and* or *because*. Then check in the text.

1 I live in a big house _____ I drive to the shops.
2 I'm often tired _____ we work six days a week.

C Complete the sentences with *and* or *because*.

1 My English is good _____ I study a lot.
2 I like coffee _____ I have ten cups every day.
3 I'm a waiter _____ I work in the city centre.
4 I don't walk to work _____ it's ten kilometres.

6A Write a blog entry about your life. Use *and* and *because*. Write 50–70 words.

B Work in pairs and read your blogs. What is the same and what is different?

GRAMMAR present simple questions

7A Complete the tables with *do* or *don't*.

_____	you	have	a car?
Yes, I _____.		No, I _____.	

Where What		you	live? study?

B ▶ 4.2 Listen and circle the correct intonation.

A: Do you live in a flat? ¹↗ ↘
B: Yes, I do. ²↗ ↘ And you? ³↗ ↘
A: No, I don't. ⁴↗ ↘ I live in a house. ⁵↗ ↘

C Work in pairs and practise the conversation.

▶ page 124 **LANGUAGEBANK**

PRACTICE

8A Put the words in order to make questions.

1 cats / like / you / Do ?
   Do you like cats?
2 films / like / you / Do / American ?
3 have / Do / a / you / dictionary ?
4 you / like / Do / cola ?
5 sports / like / do / you / What ?
6 live / Where / you / do ?

B Work in pairs and take turns. Ask and answer the questions.

SPEAKING

9A Work alone and complete the sentences.

1 I like … *I like Chinese food.*
2 I don't like …
3 I study …
4 I have …
5 I don't have …

B Work in pairs and take turns. Ask and answer questions.
A: Do you like Chinese food?
B: Yes, I do.
A: Me, too.

C Tell the class the things that are the same for you and your partner.
We both like Chinese food …

> ► **GRAMMAR** | present simple: *he/she/it* ► **VOCABULARY** | time phrases ► **HOW TO** | talk about people's lives

Me and my avatar

Rebecca

In real life, Rebecca Green is a normal twenty-eight-year-old. Rebecca lives in London and works in a bank. She has a small flat one hour from London by train, and she doesn't have a car because it costs a lot of money. She says she likes her job, but she also says she wants a new job, a new life. She watches TV every night, and goes shopping with her friends at the weekend. She doesn't like sport.

In her other life, Rebecca is LittleMe – that's her Second Life avatar. LittleMe lives in a tree house and is a singer at a club. She drives a sports car and has a boyfriend, Rex05. He plays guitar in LittleMe's band. She doesn't know his real life name or identity.

LittleMe

José

In real life, José Delgado is a normal thirty-year-old. He lives in a small flat in Chicago and he works in a supermarket. He doesn't drive but he likes cycling and always cycles to work. José speaks Spanish because his family is from Ecuador, and he teaches Spanish at a language school on Saturday mornings. José doesn't have a lot of friends in Chicago, so in the evenings he plays computer games and at the weekend he phones and emails his old friends from Ecuador or he watches football on TV.

In his other life, José is Rex05 – that's his Second Life avatar. He lives in a big flat and plays guitar in a band at a club. He drives a sports car and has a girlfriend, LittleMe – she sings in the band. He doesn't know her real life name or identity.

Rex05

READING

1A Look at the photos of two people and their avatars. Answer the questions.

1 Who do you think works in a bank?
2 Who do you think sings in a band?
3 Who do you think drives a sports car?
4 Who do you think speaks Spanish?
5 Who do you think lives in a tree house?
6 Who do you think plays guitar in a band?

B Work in pairs and check your answers. Student A: read Rebecca's text. Student B: read José's text. Two answers are <u>not</u> in your text.

C Work with other students. Student As: check your answers. Student Bs: check your answers.

2A Work in pairs. Student A: you are Rebecca. Complete the questions to ask José. Student B: you are José. Complete the questions to ask Rebecca.

1 Where / live? *Where do you live?*
2 What / your job?
3 drive?
4 What / do / in the evening?
5 What / do / at the weekend?
6 What / your avatar's name?

B Work in pairs. Ask and answer questions 1–6. Find three differences between each person in their real life and in their Second Life.

C Work with other students and discuss. Are Rebecca and José a good couple? What about LittleMe and Rex05?

GRAMMAR present simple: *he/she/it*

3A Underline the verbs in the sentences.

1 Rebecca lives in London.
2 She has a small flat.
3 She doesn't have a car.

B Complete the table. Use the sentences above and the text in Exercise 1B to help.

+	He She It	work___ watch___ cost___	in a supermarket. TV every night. a lot of money.
	He	ha___	a small flat.
–	He	_____ know	her name.
	She	_____ have	a house.

C Complete the rules.

Rules:

1 *He/she/it* + verb + _____.
2 With *have*: use *he/she/it* + _____.
3 With verbs ending *-ch* and *-o*: use verb + _____.

4A ▶ 4.3 Listen and write the verbs.

B Which two verbs have the sound /ɪz/ at the end? Listen and check, then listen and repeat.

➡ page 124 **LANGUAGEBANK**

PRACTICE

5A Complete the text with the correct form of the verb in brackets.

My real name's Dean and my avatar, NeoStar, is very different from me. He ¹_____ (live) in a beautiful house, but I ²_____ (live) in a small flat. I ³_____ (work) in a school but he ⁴_____ (not have) a job and he ⁵_____ (have) a lot of free time. He ⁶_____ (know) a lot of people and in the evenings, he ⁷_____ (go) out to clubs with his friends. I ⁸_____ (not know) many people here and I ⁹_____ (not go) out because it ¹⁰_____ (cost) a lot. He ¹¹_____ (like) his life, but I ¹²_____ (not like) my life.

B Work in pairs and close your books. Write what you remember about Dean and NeoStar.

SPEAKING

6 Work in pairs. Student A: turn to page 149. Student B: turn to page 153.

VOCABULARY days; time phrases

7A Number the days of the week in order.

Saturday ___
Thursday ___
Wednesday ___
Sunday ___
Tuesday ___
Friday ___
Monday *1*

B ▶ 4.4 Listen and check. Then listen and repeat.

8A Complete the phrases with *in, on, at* or *every*.

1 *every* day, week, month, Monday, weekend, morning
2 _____ the weekend, night
3 _____ the morning, the afternoon, the evening
4 _____ Monday, Wednesday

B Underline the correct alternative.

1 I have coffee *in/on/every* morning.
2 I don't have coffee *in/on/every* the evening.
3 I meet my friends *in/at/on* Fridays and Saturdays.
4 I don't work *on/at/every* the weekend.
5 I study English *on/at/every* day.

C Change the sentences above so that they are true for you. Then work in pairs and compare your answers.

A: I have tea every morning.
B: I don't. I have coffee.

VOCABULARY events

1A Match the words in the box with events A–F. Do **not** use one of the words.

film   party   play   concert   match
festival   lesson

B Work in pairs and take turns. Ask and answer about the events in the box.
A: Do you like concerts?
B: No, I don't. What about you?
A: I don't like concerts, but I like plays.

FUNCTION telling the time

2A ▶ 4.5 Listen to the conversations. Which event does the person ask about?

1 _music festival_
2 _____
3 _____
4 _____
5 _____
6 _____

B Listen again. Complete the conversations with a number.

Conversation 1
A: Excuse me, what time is it?
B: It's _____ o'clock.

Conversation 2
B: What time's the lesson?
A: At half past _____.

Conversation 3
A: Excuse me. What time is the film?
B: At quarter to _____ and half past _____.

Conversation 4
B: What time's the match?
A: At quarter past _____.

Conversation 5
A: What time is it now?
B: It's quarter to _____.

Conversation 6
A: What time's the concert?
B: At quarter past _____.

▶ page 124 **LANGUAGEBANK**

A

Romeo & Juliet
8th August 8.00p.m. The Globe £25

B

BBC One
2.15
World Cup Final
Full Schedule

C

New time
English lessons
Tues/Thurs
~~4.00p.m.~~ 3·30
All levels available

D

Olivia's birthday!
Come and celebrate!
FRIDAY 10P.M.–LATE

E

CINEMA LISTINGS
Movieplex – Guildford
View all cinema listings   View cinema details
View Map

Avatar III
Premiere photos

Monday	6.15	8.45	10.30
Tuesday	6.15	8.45	10.30
Wednesday	6.15	8.45	10.30
Thursday	6.15	8.45	10.30

Friday 23rd December 7.15p.m.
The O2
LIVE!
U2

F

3A ▶ 4.6 Listen and repeat the times.

A

B

C

D

B Work in pairs and take turns. Student A: ask the time. Student B: say the time.

⟱ page 142 **PHOTOBANK**

LEARN TO check times

4A Look at the conversation. How does the speaker check the time? Underline three sentences.

A: What time is the concert?
B: At quarter past seven.
A: Sorry? When?
B: Quarter past seven.
A: Quarter past seven. Thanks.

B ▶ 4.7 Look at the intonation in the questions. Then listen and repeat.

Sorry?   When?

speakout TIP

Check you understand people's answers. Repeat the information to check you understand.

C Work in pairs and take turns. Student A: say one of the times below. Student B: check the time and write it.

8:15
9:30
5:30
7:30
7:45
11:30

A: Quarter to eight.
B: Sorry? When?
A: Quarter to eight.
B: Quarter to eight. Thanks.

SPEAKING

5A Work in pairs. Student A: look at the information below. Ask Student B to come to the events. Student B: turn to page 149.

Saturday	Sunday
10.15a.m. – film	
	1.45p.m. – play
9.30p.m. – party	

A: Let's go to a film on Saturday!
B: What time is it?
A: It's at quarter past ten.
B: OK!

B Write the events and times that Student B suggests.

DVD PREVIEW

1A Which words in the box are in the photos?

| river | falls/waterfall | fish | bridge | boat |

B Look at the map. Which countries does the Mekong River cross? Where are the Khone Falls?

Mekong River
THAILAND LAOS
Khone Falls
CAMBODIA
VIETNAM

C Match the opposites.

1 wet   a) easy
2 fresh   b) safe
3 difficult   c) dead
4 dangerous   d) dry
5 alive   e) frozen

2 Read the programme information. What are three good things and two bad things about rivers? Who is the man in the photo?

BBC Human Planet: Rivers

The BBC series *Human Planet* is about the lifestyles of people around the world. This programme looks at the life of people who live by rivers.

Rivers are alive. They change with the four seasons. Rivers give us many things: fresh water, food, and ways to go from place to place. But life on a river is sometimes difficult and dangerous.

Sam Niang and his family live by the Mekong River near the Khone Falls. This is the story of a day in his life in the rainy season.

▶ DVD VIEW

3A Watch the DVD. Tick the correct alternative in each group.

A family	goes to the market	and buys a fish.
A man	walks to the river	and catches a fish.
A woman	crosses a bridge	and catches two fish.

B Work in pairs. Watch the DVD again and underline the correct alternative.

1 The world is a place of extremes: hot and *frozen/ cold,* wet and *fresh/dry.*

2 In winter, the dry season, the Falls *are/aren't* very big but in summer, the *rainy/wet* season, they're very dangerous.

3 He crosses the river on a *simple/small* bridge. It's very, very *difficult/dangerous.* A man falls and he's *frozen/dead.*

4 Sam Niang fishes. He catches his family's *lunch/ dinner.*

5 Tomorrow is a *new/hot* day and Sam Niang will go back to the *river/bridge* to catch fish for his family again.

C Work in pairs and discuss. How do you think Sam Niang feels? Choose words from the box.

| afraid   happy   angry   tired   hot   surprised |
| hungry   bored |

speakout a favourite season

4A Think about your favourite season. Why do you like it? Think about:

- holidays
- clothes
- activities
- weather

B ▶ 4.8 Listen to someone talking about her favourite season. Tick the topics she talks about.

C Listen again and tick the key phrases you hear.

keyphrases

My favourite season is (spring/summer/autumn/winter)

I like it because it's …

It's a beautiful season.

I don't like the (summer/winter) because I don't like (very hot/very cold) weather.

My favourite holiday is in (autumn).

(The/My family/Friends) come(s) together for (a big dinner/a party).

5A Work in pairs. Practise talking about your favourite season. Use the key phrases to help.

B Work in groups and take turns. One student: talk about your favourite season. Other students: listen and ask one question.

writeback a forum reply

6A Read the message from a forum and answer the questions.

1 What is Kylie's favourite season?
2 Why?
3 What is the problem with this season?

> **? Open Question**
> **What is your favourite season and why?**
> Asked by Jay Green
>
> My favourite season is _____. I like it because I love the cold mornings and the frozen countryside. The trees and the roads are beautiful … all white and fresh. I know that travelling is difficult but it's not a problem for me. I walk everywhere! I also like _____ because I go skiing in the mountains.
>
> Answers (9)

B Write a reply to the forum about your favourite season. Use 40–60 words and remember to use *and*, *but* and *because*. Answer the questions below.

1 What is your favourite season?
2 Why do you like it?
3 What are the problems?

47

VERB PHRASES

1A Cross out the word or phrase that is <u>not</u> correct.

1 I like *cats / people / ~~late~~*.
2 You work *in pairs / the city / in an office*.
3 We go *university / to English lessons / to the gym*.
4 They have *a car / a problem / hungry*.
5 You live *a flat / in Hong Kong / alone*.
6 We study *Spanish / five hours a week / bored*.
7 I drive *a sports car / work / a taxi*.
8 They do *tennis / sport / homework*.

B Think of a good friend. What is the same about you and your friend? Write three sentences using the verbs above.

Sonia is a good friend from university. We both like the cinema. We are twenty-three and we work in the city.

C Work in pairs and take turns. Read your sentences.

PRESENT SIMPLE: *I/YOU/WE/THEY*

2A Use the table to write four questions.

Do	you	like … ?
	your friends	work … ?
		read … ?
	you and your friends	do … ?
		live … ?
	the other students in the class	watch … ?
		have … ?
		go … ?

1 *Do you and your friends watch English films?*

B Work in pairs and take turns. Ask and answer your questions.

PRESENT SIMPLE: *HE/SHE/IT*

3A Complete the sentences.

1 He / not / work / hotel
He doesn't work in a hotel.
2 She / live / in a flat
3 He / not / like / hamburgers
4 She / have / a brother
5 He / not / like / shopping
6 She / do / sport / at the weekend

B Work in pairs. Change *he/she* in sentences 1–6 above. Write the names of students in your class.

1 *Abel doesn't work in a hotel.*
2 *Patrizia lives in a flat.*

C Check the information with the students.
A: Abel, do you work in a hotel?
B: No, I don't.

DAYS; TIME PHRASES

4A Write the days of the week.

Mo	Tu	We	Th	Fr	Sa	Su

Monday

B Match the times 1–6 with the phrases a)–f).

1 Monday, Monday, Monday *c)*
2 9a.m.
3 Saturday and Sunday
4 3p.m.
5 9p.m.
6 Monday–Sunday

a) at the weekend
b) in the evening
c) every Monday
d) in the morning
e) every day
f) in the afternoon

C Write something you do at the times in Exercise 4B.

I do sport every Monday.

D Work in pairs and take turns. Student A: say an activity. Student B: guess the time.
A: I do sport. *B: In the evening?*
A: No. *B: Every Monday?*
A: Yes!

EVENTS

5A Add vowels to complete the events.

1 f _i_ lm
2 c__nc__rt
3 l__ss__n
4 p__rty
5 pl__y
6 f__st__v__l
7 m__tch

B Work in pairs and take turns. Student A: choose an event and say a word to help. Student B: guess the event.
A: Shakespeare.
B: A play?
A: Yes!

TELLING THE TIME

6A Write the times in words.

1 5.45 *Quarter to six.*
2 12.30 _____
3 7.15 _____
4 3.00 _____
5 3.45 _____
6 11.15 _____

B Write six times in numbers.

C Work in pairs and take turns. Student A: read your times. Student B: write them in numbers. Then check.
A: Half past three.
B: (writes) 2.30
A: (checks) No, it's 3.30.

LISTENING AND GRAMMAR

1A Match the words in the box with the icons.

> cafés *F*   clothes   films   people
> places   websites

B Work in pairs and take turns. Student A: choose one icon and give an example. Student B: say the icon.

A: The King's Speech.
B: Films.
A: Correct.
B: Chris, my son.
A: People.

2A ▶ R2.1 Listen to a woman talking about her favourite things and people. Number the icons in Exercise 1A in order.

B Listen again. How many things or people does she talk about for each icon?

Cafés ____
Clothes ____
Films ____
People __3__
Places ____
Websites ____

3A Complete the sentences.

1 Alicia / be / Beth / sister
   Alicia is Beth's sister.
2 William / say / Alicia / be / beautiful
3 Beth / know / Keith / from university
4 Beth / Monique / be / not / friends
5 Beth / have / red party dress
6 She / like / the BBC website
7 She / go / the Gelatino Café / every day

B Work in pairs. Which sentence in Exercise 3A is false? Check audio script Review 2.1 on page 156.

SPEAKING

4A Complete 1, 2 and 3 in the table with three words in the box.

> people   places   restaurants   cafés   clothes   music   films   animals

My favourites		
1 _____	2 _____	3 _____

B Complete your table with three things or people for each group.

C Work with other students and take turns. Ask and answer about your favourite things and people.

A: What are your groups?
B: Places, clothes, music.
A: OK. What are your favourite places?
B: Rome, Milan and London.
A: Oh, why?
B: I like cities. Rome is very old and beautiful …

REVIEW 2: UNITS 3–4

READING AND GRAMMAR

5A Read the descriptions of Keith and Alicia. What are their jobs?

My friend Keith works alone. He works from three in the afternoon to twelve at night every day, but he doesn't have time to stop or to eat. He meets people from many different countries. He goes to and from the airport five or six times every day and has about twenty different customers in his car. He also drives people around the city and knows it very well. Keith likes his job but he says he doesn't like working in the evenings and he gets very tired at the end of his day.

My sister Alicia's job isn't very difficult. On a typical day, she sits at her desk from nine to five and welcomes people when they come in. She checks their names, nationalities and car numbers and then gives them their room key. What else? She answers the phone, reads and writes emails and takes people's money when they go. She says she likes her job because every day is different but she doesn't like her work clothes: a white shirt and red trousers.

B Who says 1–8 below? Keith (K) or Alicia (A)?

1 No, I don't have special clothes for work. *K*
2 No, I don't work in an office.
3 Yes, I do. I speak on the phone a lot.
4 Yes, I use a computer in my job.
5 No, I don't work in the evenings.
6 Yes, I drive a lot in my job.

C Look again at the answers in Exercise 5B. Write the questions.

1 Do you have special clothes for work?

D Work in pairs. Compare your day with Keith's and Alicia's.

Keith drives in his job, but I don't. Alicia works at a desk and I do, too.

SPEAKING

6A Work in groups. Write the names of ten jobs.

B Work in groups and take turns. Student A: choose a job. Other students: ask questions to find the job.
B: Do you work in an office? **A:** *No, I don't.*
C: Do you work in a hospital? **A:** *Yes, I do.*

SOUNDS: /s/ AND /z/

7A ▶ R2.2 Listen to the sounds and the words. Then listen and repeat.

/s/	/z/
cake**s**	coffee**s**

B ▶ R2.3 Listen and put the words in the box in the correct group. Then listen and repeat.

~~tea**s**~~ ~~sparkling~~ ha**s** **s**andwich euro**s** **s**port drive**s** thi**s**

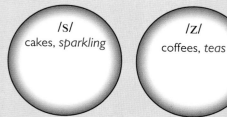

/s/
cakes, *sparkling*

/z/
coffees, *teas*

8A Work in pairs. Circle the word with a different *s* sound.

1 (this,) these, those
2 Jack's, Pat's, Tom's
3 sweater, trousers, hats
4 it's, he's, she's
5 books, bags, cups
6 goes, does, likes

B ▶ R2.4 Listen and check. Then listen and repeat.

C Complete the rules with /s/ or /z/ for the pronunciation of *s*.

Rules:
1 At the beginning of words: _____
2 At the end of words, after /k/, /t/ and /p/: _____
3 At the end of words, after /d/, /m/, /g/, /v/, /l/, /n/: _____

9A Underline sixteen examples of the letter *s* in the sentences.

   /s/
1 My **s**on lives near the sea and the mountains.
2 The lamps and the clocks are in the rooms near the beds.
3 Can I have six eggs, please?
4 Sue emails her parents on Sundays.

B How is the *s* pronounced in each word? Write /s/ or /z/. Use the rules in Exercise 8C to help.

C ▶ R2.5 Listen and check. Then listen and repeat.

UNIT 5

SPEAKING
> Discuss bad habits
> Talk about what you eat
> Talk about your routines
> Ask for tourist information

LISTENING
> Listen to people say what drives them crazy
> Listen to a tourist asking questions
> Watch a BBC programme about Doctor Who

READING
> Read what a sportsman and model eat
> Read about someone's morning routine

WRITING
> Use linkers to sequence
> Write a forum entry

BBC content
> Video podcast: What do you usually do at the weekend?
> DVD: Doctor Who

routines

▶ Bad habits p52

▶ Superman and supermodel p54

▶ When does it open? p56

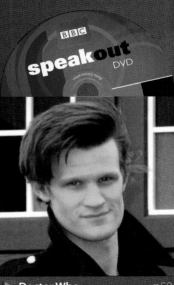
▶ Doctor Who p58

VOCABULARY daily routines

1A ▶ 5.1 Listen and match the sounds with the verbs in the box.

> get up *1*   go to bed   have dinner
> go to work   have lunch   get home
> have breakfast

B Work in pairs and take turns. Ask and answer about your daily routines.

A: *What time do you get up?*
B: *I get up at seven o'clock. And you?*

IIII▶ page 142–3 **PHOTOBANK**

LISTENING

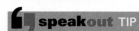

speakout TIP

Practice helps you to remember. Write seven sentences about your daily routine. Practise saying them every day.

2A Work in pairs and look at the photos. Who is angry and why?

B ▶ 5.2 Listen to the conversations and underline the correct alternative.

1 She talks about her *husband/daughter/ neighbour*.

2 She talks about her *boyfriend/her brother/a person at work*.

3 He talks about *a person at work/his brother /his neighbour*.

C Listen again and tick one true sentence. Correct the false sentences.

1 Clara has a job.
   Clara doesn't have a job.

2 Clara talks to her parents.

3 Julio listens to Paula.

4 Paula doesn't talk about her problems.

5 Wayne's neighbour works at night.

6 Wayne gets up at eight o'clock.

D Work in pairs. Do you have these problems with family, friends, neighbours or people at work?

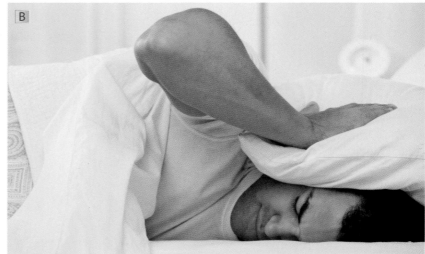

GRAMMAR present simple questions: *he/she/it*

3A Complete the tables with *does* and *doesn't*.

What		it	mean?
What time When	_____	she he	get up? go to bed?

		she he	have a job? play loud music?
Yes, he/she _____.		No, he/she _____.	

B ▶ 5.3 Look at the pronunciation of *does he/ she/ it* in the questions. Then listen and repeat.

1 What does it mean?
   /dəzɪt/

2 When does he go to bed?
   /dəzɪ/

3 Does she have a job?
   /dəʃɪ/

IIII▶ page 126 **LANGUAGEBANK**

C

PRACTICE

4 Add *does* in four places in each conversation.

           does
1 **A:** What time ⋏ Mike come home in the evenings?
   B: At about eight o'clock.
   A: So, he play with the children?
   B: No, he doesn't. They go to bed at seven.
   A: And he work at the weekends?
   B: Yes, he, or he goes out and plays tennis!

2 **A:** Ana, your sister phone you on your birthday?
   B: No, she doesn't.
   A: When she phone you?
   B: On <u>her</u> birthday because she wants money!
   A: Really? So it drive you crazy?
   B: Yes, it.

5A Complete the questions with the verbs in the box.

~~like~~ study go watch have listen do read

1 (he) _____*Does he like*_____ English lessons?
2 (she) _____ her homework every day?
3 (he) _____ a job?
4 (she) _____ at university?
5 (your teacher) _____ a newspaper every day?
6 (you) _____ to the radio?
7 (your sister) _____ DVDs a lot?
8 (he) _____ to parties a lot?

B Choose five questions from Exercise 5A. Add the names of students in your class.

1 Does Marcus like English lessons?

C Work in pairs and take turns to ask and answer. If you don't know, ask the person or say *I don't know.*

A: *Does Marcus like English lessons?*
B: *I don't know. Excuse me, Marcus. Do you like English lessons?*
C: *Yes, I do.*
B: *Yes, he does. Does Rachel …*

SPEAKING

6A Work in pairs. Ask and answer the questions in the quiz below. Put a tick when your partner answers yes.

B Change partners. Ask and answer the questions about your first partner.
A: *Who is your person?*
B: *Oscar.*
A: *OK. Does he talk a lot and not listen?*

10 bad habits that drive people crazy

Do you …

- ◉ talk a lot and not listen? ☐
- ◉ answer the phone all the time? ☐
- ◉ stay in the bathroom for hours? ☐
- ◉ talk in films? ☐
- ◉ eat on trains? ☐
- ◉ sing in the bathroom? ☐
- ◉ copy other people's work (e.g. homework)? ☐
- ◉ play very loud music in the car or at home? ☐
- ◉ smoke? ☐
- ◉ drive very fast? ☐

VOCABULARY food

1A Match the words with photos A–L.

1	pasta _K_	7	vegetables ____
2	steak ____	8	bread ____
3	chicken ____	9	cereal ____
4	chips ____	10	eggs ____
5	fish ____	11	cheese ____
6	fruit ____	12	sugar ____

B Write the number of syllables (1, 2 or 3) next to each word.

1 pasta 2

C ► 5.4 Listen and check. Then listen and repeat.

2 Work in pairs and take turns to ask questions. What food do you both like?

A: I like steak. Do you?
B: No, I don't. Do you like pasta?
A: Yes, I do.

▶ page 143 **PHOTOBANK**

READING

3A Discuss in pairs. What do you know about the two people in the photos? What food do you think they eat?

B Read the texts and answer the questions. Write M (Michael), H (Heidi) or MH (Michael and Heidi).

Who ...

1 eats a lot? *MH*
2 talks about steak and chicken?
3 thinks it's important to eat healthy food?
4 has a big breakfast?
5 doesn't eat a lot of vegetables and fruit?
6 eats a lot of Italian food?

Michael Phelps
Swimmer

I love food! I need about 12,000 calories a day, so I have a big breakfast – usually three fried egg sandwiches, a five-egg omelette and three pieces of French toast* with sugar. For lunch I have the same thing every day; I always have a big plate of pasta, and two very big cheese sandwiches. For dinner I have another big plate of pasta and a whole pizza. I don't often eat vegetables or fruit.

*toast: cooked bread

Heidi Klum
Supermodel

I'm never hungry because I eat a lot. In the morning, I usually have a big breakfast with fruit and cereal, and for lunch I eat a lot of vegetables, but in the evening I only have a small dinner. I often eat chicken, but I don't often eat red meat (I have steak maybe once a week) and I sometimes eat fish, maybe two or three times a week. I never eat chips because of my job. It's important for me to look good and be healthy.

C Read the texts again. Is this the food for Michael or Heidi?

	Mon	Tue	Wed	Thu	Fri	Sat	Sun
chicken	✓		✓		✓	✓	
chips							
fish		✓		✓			
fruit	✓	✓	✓	✓		✓	✓
pizza							
steak							✓
vegetables	✓	✓	✓	✓	✓		

D Discuss in pairs. Is your diet similar to Michael's or Heidi's?

GRAMMAR adverbs of frequency

4A Underline the words in the box in the texts on page 54.

> sometimes always never often
> not often usually

B Put the words in the box in the correct place on the line below. Use the texts and the chart in Exercise 3 to help you.

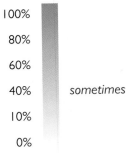

100%
80%
60%
40%   *sometimes*
10%
0%

C ▶ 5.5 Listen and underline the stress in the adverbs. Then listen and repeat.

always

D Look at sentences 1–3. Underline the correct alternative in the rules.

1 I'm **never** hungry because I eat a lot.

2 I **usually** have a big breakfast …

3 I **don't often** eat red meat.

> Rules:
> 1 The adverb goes *before/after* the verb *be*.
> 2 The adverb goes *before/after* other verbs.

▶ page 126 **LANGUAGEBANK**

PRACTICE

5A Put the words in the correct order to make sentences.

1 have / usually / I / Fridays / on / fish

1 I usually have fish on Fridays.

2 eat / never / I / sweets

3 hungry / I'm / never

4 eat / often / chicken / I

5 home / dinner / for / usually / I'm

6 fruit / eat / don't / I / often

7 have / sometimes / I / lunch / for / vegetables

8 I / eat / Sundays / steak / always / on

B Work in pairs. Which sentences are true for you? Change the other sentences to make them true.

SPEAKING

6A Read the sentences below. Complete them with *always* (A), *usually* (U), *sometimes* (S), *not often* (NO) and *never* (N).

In the morning, I …
- ○ have a coffee before breakfast.
- ○ have a big breakfast.
- ○ make a sandwich for lunch.
- ○ read my emails.
- ○ drive to work/school.

In the evening, I …
- ○ cook dinner for my family.
- ○ eat after eight o'clock.
- ○ watch about two hours' TV.
- ○ go out with friends.
- ○ have a hot drink before I go to bed.

B Work in pairs and compare your answers. Find two things the same.

A: I never have a coffee before breakfast. What about you?
B: I never drink coffee.

WRITING linkers to sequence

7A Read the description. Is it similar to your morning?

My morning

Every day I get up at six. First, I make a black coffee, and I read my emails. Then I have breakfast and listen to the radio. I usually have cereal and coffee but I sometimes have toast and an egg. After that, I often read the news online. Finally, at half past eight I go to work. I always walk to work because it's only fifteen minutes to my office. At work I have another coffee and sometimes a cake.

B Read the description again and number the linkers in order.

> then first *1* finally after that

C Which linker does <u>not</u> have a comma after it?

8A Write a description of your typical morning. Use linkers and write 60–80 words.

B Read other students' descriptions. Are they similar to your morning?

| ▶ **FUNCTION** \| asking for information | ▶ **VOCABULARY** \| hotel services | ▶ **LEARN TO** \| show interest |

VOCABULARY hotel services

1A Look at the photos. Which services in the box are in photos A–D?

| restaurant   gym   café   gift shop
money exchange   hairdresser's
swimming pool   guided tour |

B Match the services from the box with activities 1–8.

1 have dinner *restaurant*
2 change money
3 get a haircut
4 do exercise
5 have a coffee
6 go swimming
7 buy gifts
8 see the town

C Discuss in pairs. Which two services are important in a hotel? Which two aren't important?

FUNCTION asking for information

2A ▶ 5.6 Listen to the conversations. Which four services does the woman ask about?

1 _____gym_____
2 _____
3 _____
4 _____

B Listen again. Find and correct the five mistakes in the woman's notes.

gym: 6a.m.–9p.m.,
closes: 12–1

breakfast: 6.30–9.00 – in
café

hairdresser's: 10–6;
Tuesdays to 8p.m;
closes Mondays.

guided tour: 9a.m. and
2p.m. €50.

3A ▶ 5.7 Complete the sentences. Then listen and check.

1 When does the gym *open*?
2 It _____ from 6a.m. to 10p.m.
3 What _____ is breakfast?
4 From half past six _____ nine o'clock.
5 _____ you have a hairdresser's in the hotel?
6 Yes, it opens _____ day except Monday.
7 When _____ the tour leave?
8 It _____ at 9a.m. and at 3p.m.
9 How much does it _____?
10 _____ costs fifteen euros.

B Listen again and underline the stressed words. Then listen and repeat.
1 *When* does the *gym* *open*?

⫸ page 126 **LANGUAGEBANK**

4A Complete the conversation.

Student A | Student B

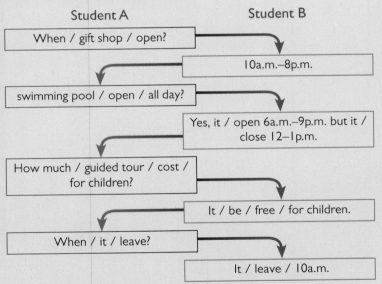

When / gift shop / open?

10a.m.–8p.m.

swimming pool / open / all day?

Yes, it / open 6a.m.–9p.m. but it / close 12–1p.m.

How much / guided tour / cost / for children?

It / be / free / for children.

When / it / leave?

It / leave / 10a.m.

B Work in pairs and take turns. Practise the conversation.

LEARN TO show interest

5A ▶ 5.8 Listen to parts of the conversation. Number the words in the order you hear them.

Great.   Oh, good.   That's good.   Lovely.   *1*   That's great.
Wonderful.

speakout TIP

When someone gives information, we often say *Great, Lovely*, etc. to show interest or say *Thank you*. What do you say in your language?

B ▶ 5.9 Listen to the intonation. Which person is interested?

1 Great.   2 Great.

C Work in pairs and take turns. Student A: say a phrase. Student B: say *interested* or *not interested*.

A: Oh, good.   **B:** Not interested.

SPEAKING

6A Work in pairs. You are tourists at a hotel in Prague. Make questions about the times and/or the prices.

You want to:
• change money.
• have coffee at Café Slavia or Café Milena.
• have lunch at the hotel.
• go on a guided tour of Prague.
• go to the opera.
What time does the money exchange open?

B Work with a new partner. Student A: you are the tourist. Ask Student B your questions and write the answers. Student B: turn to page 150 and answer the questions.

C Change roles. Student A: turn to page 153 and answer the questions. Student B: ask your questions and write the answers.

D Check your partner's information. Is it correct?

5.4 DOCTOR WHO

DVD PREVIEW

1A Match the words in the box with photos A–F.

> The London Eye *F* Big Ben fish fingers
> custard The O2 Stadium beans

B Read the programme information and answer the questions.

1 Where is Doctor Who from?
2 What's the name of his time machine?
3 What's the Doctor's problem?

BBC Doctor Who

Doctor Who is the number one science fiction television programme of all time. The Doctor isn't from this world. He's an alien. He travels in time and space in his time machine, the TARDIS, a blue 1950s British police box.

In this episode the Doctor has a new body. He's very hungry and a little girl gives him food. But what food does he like? He doesn't know.

DVD VIEW

2A Watch the DVD. Tick the items in the DVD. Which item is not in the DVD?

1 Doctor Who	6 an English house
2 The London Eye	7 custard
3 Big Ben	8 a banana
4 the TARDIS	9 fish fingers
5 The O2 Stadium	10 beans

B Work in pairs and underline the correct alternative. Then watch the DVD again to check your answers.

1 'Can I have an *carrot/apple*? All I can think about … *carrots/apples*. I love *carrots/apples*.'

2 'No, no, no, I love *yoghurt/custard*. *Yoghurt's/Custard's* my favourite. Give me *yoghurt/custard*.'

3 Ah. You see? *Carrots/Beans*. *Carrots/Beans* are evil. Bad, bad *carrots/beans*.

4 A: I've got some *carrots/apples*.
  B: *Carrots/Apples*? Are you insane? No, wait, hang on, I know what I need, I need, I need, I need …, fish fingers and *yoghurt/custard*.

C Work in pairs. How do they feel? Write D (the Doctor) or G (girl) or N (no-one).

1 afraid	5 happy
2 unhappy	6 angry
3 surprised	7 tired
4 bored	

![BBC]

speakout desert island food

3A Read the food forum and write your list.

You have 10 years on a desert island. The island has fresh water but no food. What types of food and drink do you take with you? The maximum is 5 types of food and 2 drinks. Send us your list!

B ▶ 5.10 Listen to a woman talking about her list. What food and drink does she talk about?

C Listen again and tick the key phrases you hear.

keyphrases

What's on your list?

Number (one/two/three) on my list is …

It's important to have …

I really like …

It's (good/bad) for you …

Do you really like … ?

Me too.

Really?

What about drinks?

I don't like (it/fruit/eggs)

I like (it/fruit/eggs) too.

4A Work in pairs and take turns to talk about your lists. Use the key phrases to help.

B Work in groups and take turns. One student: talk about your list. Other students: listen and ask one question.

writeback a forum entry

5A Read the reply to the forum question. Then work in pairs and discuss the questions.

1 Are these things on your list?

2 Which things on the list <u>don't</u> you like?

My food is very simple because I don't cook, and I love sandwiches.

Here's my list:

bread – I eat sandwiches every day, and I need bread for sandwiches.

cheese – A cheese sandwich is easy to make.

sausages – I think meat is important, and I love sausages. Sausages are also good in a sandwich.

apples – I don't like apples but they're good for you. Apples are good with cheese too.

tomatoes – They're my favourite food, and great on sandwiches!

coffee – I start every day with a black coffee.

orange juice – Very important for vitamin C!

B Write your list and give one reason for each item on your list.

DAILY ROUTINES

1A Add vowels to complete the daily routines.

1 g_o_ t_ _b_d
2 h_v_ br_ _kf_st
3 g_t _p
4 g_t h_m_
5 g_ t_ w_rk
6 h_v_ l_nch
7 h_v_ d_nn_r

B Work in pairs and take turns. Cover the verbs. Student A: say the first routine people do every day. Student B: repeat the first routine and say the next routine.

A: get up
B: get up, have breakfast

PRESENT SIMPLE: QUESTIONS

2A Complete the questions.

1 When / he / get up?
   When does he get up?
2 she / like / coffee / or / tea?
   _____
3 What time / he / go / to work?
   _____
4 What / she / have / for lunch?
   _____
5 he / have / a car?
   _____
6 When / she / get home?
   _____
7 she / study / at the weekend?
   _____
8 he / phone / you / every day?
   _____

B Work in pairs and take turns. Student A: ask questions. Student B: answer about a person in your family or a friend.

A: Who is your person?
B: My wife, Vanessa.
A: OK. When does she get up?

FOOD

3A Put the letters in the correct order to make food words. The first letter is underlined.

1 g<u>s</u>eg eggs
2 e<u>c</u>rela
3 ea<u>d</u>r<u>b</u>
4 <u>r</u>ugas
5 is<u>p</u>h<u>c</u>
6 <u>k</u>eat<u>s</u>
7 h<u>k</u>eicnc
8 u<u>f</u>tir
9 e<u>c</u>eseh
10 s<u>p</u>aat
11 h<u>s</u>f<u>i</u>
12 <u>v</u>ealbeetgs

B Write three foods in each circle.

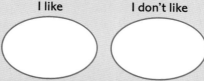

I like   I don't like

I don't eat

C Work in pairs and take turns. Student A: say one of your foods. Student B: guess if Student A likes it, doesn't like it or doesn't eat it.

A: Steak.
B: You don't like it.
A: No, I don't eat it.

ADVERBS OF FREQUENCY

4A Find and correct the mistakes. One sentence is correct.

1 We speak English together always in class.
2 I usually do my homework.
3 I'm late never for English lessons.
4 I not often watch English videos.
5 My English teacher says often 'Good!'
6 I read an online English newspaper never.

B Tick the sentences that are true for you. Change the others to make them true. Then compare with a partner.

1 *We don't always speak English together in class. We sometimes speak Italian.*

HOTEL SERVICES

5 Find and circle eight hotel services.

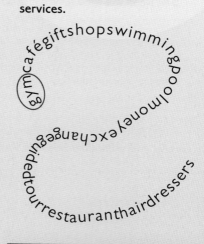

ASKING FOR INFORMATION

6A Look at the times of the hotel services. Complete questions 1–4.

1 What *time* _____ the gym close?
2 When _____ the café open?
3 _____ does the gift shop open _____ Mondays?
4 _____ does the swimming pool open and close?

B Work alone. Complete the timetable a)–d) with times.

Hotel services

a) **gym** 8a.m.– _____ Mon–Sat (~~Sun~~)
b) **café** _____ –10p.m. Mon–Sun
c) **gift shop** 11a.m.–7p.m. Tue–Sun (~~Mon~~)
d) **swimming pool** _____ – _____ (Mon–Sun)

C Work in pairs and take turns. Ask and answer questions 1–4.

UNIT
6

SPEAKING
❯ Find differences in lifestyles
❯ Ask and answer questions about transport
❯ Buy a ticket for travel
❯ Talk about travel in your country

LISTENING
❯ Listen to a man stuck at a station
❯ Listen to someone buy a bus ticket
❯ Watch a BBC programme about rush hour in India

READING
❯ Read some fun facts about transport

WRITING
❯ Start and end emails
❯ Write in a travel forum

BBC content
▣ Video podcast: How do you get to school or work?
◉ DVD: Visions of India: Rush Hour

journeys

BBC speakout DVD

▶ **No trains**   p62

▶ **Getting there**   p64

▶ **Single or return?**   p66

▶ **Rush Hour**   p68

VOCABULARY places

1A Match the words in the box with pictures A–H.

> internet café C   newsagent's   hotel
> snack bar   restaurant   pharmacy
> payphone   cash machine

A 	B
C 	D 
E 	F
G	H

B ▶ 6.1 Listen to places A–H and underline the stressed syllable(s). Then listen and repeat.
internet café

C Work in pairs and take turns. Ask and answer about the pictures in Exercise 1A.
A: What's G?
B: It's a cash machine. What's … ?

▷ page 144 **PHOTOBANK**

LISTENING

2A Look at the photo. What's the problem? Do you like train travel? What is good and what is bad about it?

B ▶ 6.2 Listen to the conversations and number the places in Exercise 1A in the order you hear them. Two places are <u>not</u> in the conversations.
payphone 1

C Listen again and underline the correct alternative.
1 The weather is *cold/bad*.
2 The man's phone is *dead/broken*.
3 The internet café *is/isn't* in the station.
4 The restaurants are *closed/expensive*.
5 The Charlotte Street Hotel is *full/expensive*.

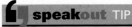
speakout TIP

Before you do an exercise, check new words. Try to guess the meaning, ask your teacher or another student or check in your dictionary.

GRAMMAR *there is/are*

3A Complete the tables with the words in the box.

> 's   Are   There   are   Is   there   aren't

+	There	[1] 's	a payphone over there.
		[2] _____	two hotels near here.
–	[3] _____	isn't	an internet café.
		[4] _____	any trains.

?	[5] _____	there	a train to Paris tonight?
	[6] _____		any restaurants in the station?

+	Yes,	[7]	is
			are.
–	No,		isn't.
			aren't.

B ▶ 6.3 Listen and check.

C Listen again and underline the main stress in each sentence. Then listen and repeat.

▷ page 128 **LANGUAGEBANK**

SPEAKING

6 Work in pairs. Student A: look at the picture on page 151. Student B: look at the picture on page 153.

WRITING starting and ending an email

7A Read the email. Is the email to the woman's manager, friend or husband?

Hi Ron,
I have good news and bad news. There aren't any trains tonight because the weather's very bad. That's the bad news. So what's the good news? I'm in a very good hotel and there's a nice restaurant, too. Yes, it's expensive, but I have the company credit card.
Give the children a goodnight kiss from me. See you tomorrow.
Love,
Clare

B Complete the table with phrases for starting and ending an email.

Hi Valentina, Best wishes, Love, Hello, Take care, Dear Jack, See you soon, Dear Mr Wilson, Regards,

	to a boyfriend/ girlfriend/ husband/wife	to a friend	to your manager
Start	Hi Valentina,	Hi Valentina,	
End		Best wishes,	Best wishes,

8A Work in pairs. Which problems often happen to you when you travel by plane?

plane is late   no planes   no ticket

you're ill   food is expensive

no passport   no restaurants

B Choose two of the problems above. Write an email from the airport to a friend or to your manager. Write about your problems.

C Read other students' emails. Which situation is *really* bad?

PRACTICE

4A Complete the sentences about a class with *There's, There are, There isn't* or *There aren't*.

1 ___There are___ three students with black shoes. (+)
2 _____ one person with a red T-shirt. (+)
3 _____ a whiteboard. (−)
4 _____ two women in this room. (+)
5 _____ a book on the teacher's desk. (+)
6 _____ any dictionaries. (−)

B Work in pairs. Which sentences are true about your class?

5A Work in pairs. Student A: write questions about places near the class. Student B: write questions about places near Student A's home.

1 snack bar?
  Is there a snack bar near here?
2 internet café?
3 pharmacy?
4 any restaurants?
5 cash machine?
6 any clothes shops?

B Work in pairs and take turns. Ask and answer the questions.

A: *Is there a snack bar near here?*
B: *Yes, there's a good snack bar. It's two minutes from here. Its name is …*

VOCABULARY transport

1A Write the transport words in the box under pictures A–H.

> ~~bus~~ train plane taxi underground
> car bike motorbike

A   *bus*   B _____   C _____

D _____   E _____

F _____   G _____   H _____

B Work in pairs and answer the questions.

1 How do you come to class?
   By bus or sometimes I walk.
2 What's your favourite type of transport?
   Motorbike.
3 What type of transport do you <u>never</u> use?
   I never use a bike.

READING

2A Read the text. Which fact is <u>not</u> true?

B Write the name of the place or transport.

1 It doesn't have any stations. *Bhutan*
2 It's the number one place for bikes.
3 In London, they're usually black.
4 It's a noisy place to play.
5 Men don't use these.
6 They have two floors and stairs.

C Work in pairs and discuss. Which facts are surprising?

It's surprising that there are taxis for women. It's a good idea.

Transport facts...

More and more people are on the move. From Moscow to Beijing, and from Amsterdam to Thailand, we look at transport facts around the world.

There are 3 million cars in Moscow and 22 pink taxis. The pink taxis are for women and the drivers are women.

There are double-decker buses in the UK, Germany, Hong Kong and Singapore. There are double-decker trains in a lot of countries including Switzerland, Australia and the USA.

4.3 million people go by subway (underground) every day in New York City.

There aren't any trains in the country of Bhutan in Asia.

In Saudi Arabia some hotels have London taxis but they are white not black.

In China people often sit in the front seat of taxis.

People usually travel around Venice by car.

In Thailand, there's an airport with a golf course in it.

Amsterdam is the bike capital of the world. 40% of travel in this city is by bike.

GRAMMAR *a/an, some, a lot of, not any*

3A Look at the sentences. Match the words in bold with pictures A–D.

1 In Thailand, there's **an** airport with a golf course in it. *B*
2 There are double-decker trains in **a lot of** countries.
3 There **aren't any** trains in the country of Bhutan.
4 In Saudi Arabia **some** hotels have London taxis.

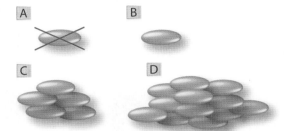

B Complete the table with *'s, are, isn't* or *aren't*.

+	There	_____	a	train at four o'clock.
		_____	some	buses this afternoon.
		_____	a lot of	taxis.
−	There	_____	an	airport here.
		_____	any	cars in the centre.

C ▶ 6.4 Listen and check.

D Listen again and underline the stressed words. Then listen and repeat.

➠ page 128 **LANGUAGEBANK**

PRACTICE

4A Underline the correct alternative.

1 There's *a/an* airport.
2 There are *some/any* stations.
3 There aren't *a lot/any* taxis.
4 There are *a lot/some* of motorbikes.
5 There isn't *a/some* bus station.
6 There are *any/some* buses at night.
7 There aren't *some/any* problems with cars in the centre.
8 There are *any/a lot of* bikes.

B Work alone. Make the sentences true for your town/city or a town/city you know.

C Work in pairs and take turns to ask questions. Student A: you are a visitor to the town/city.

A: Is there an airport?
B: Yes, there are two airports.

SPEAKING

5A Work in pairs. Student A: turn to page 150. Student B: ask questions to complete the information for Venice and London.

B: Is there a train from the airport to Venice?
A: No, there isn't.

	Venice	London (Heathrow)
train / from the airport?		
underground?		
airport bus?		
other information?		

B Change roles. Student B: answer Student A's questions about Barcelona and Edinburgh.

A: Is there a train from the airport to Barcelona?
B: Yes, there is. It's three euros.

	Barcelona	Edinburgh
train / from the airport?	€3	no
underground?	yes but not from the airport	no
airport bus?	€5	£4
other information?	taxi, €30	taxi, £15

C What's the best way to go from the airport to the centre in these four cities?

▶ **FUNCTION** | buying a ticket   ▶ **VOCABULARY** | travel   ▶ **LEARN TO** | check numbers

VOCABULARY travel

1A Work in pairs. Do you like long bus journeys? Why/Why not?

B Look at the words in the box. Which things can you see in the photos?

> passenger   ticket office   gate
> single (ticket)   return (ticket)
> monthly pass

C Work in pairs and take turns to ask and answer.
A: What's this?
B: It's a gate. What's ... ?

FUNCTION buying a ticket

2 ▶ 6.5 Listen to the conversation at a bus station and tick the correct answer.

1 She wants:
   a) a single b) a return c) two returns

2 She wants a ticket for:
   a) today b) tomorrow c) today and tomorrow

3 It costs:
   a) €25 b) €29 c) €39

4 It leaves at:
   a) 2.30 b) 2.15 c) 3.30

5 It arrives at:
   a) 3.15 b) 4.15 c) 4.45

3A ▶ 6.6 Complete the conversation. Then listen and check.

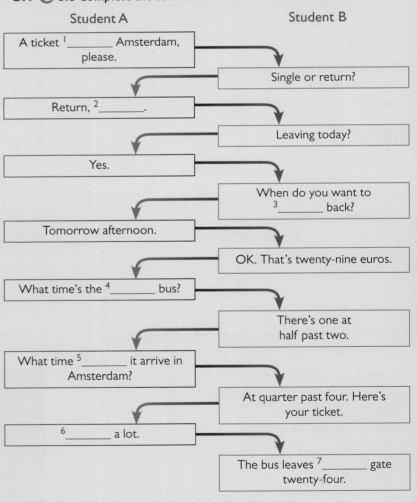

Student A   Student B

A ticket ¹_____ Amsterdam, please.

Single or return?

Return, ²_____.

Leaving today?

Yes.

When do you want to ³_____ back?

Tomorrow afternoon.

OK. That's twenty-nine euros.

What time's the ⁴_____ bus?

There's one at half past two.

What time ⁵_____ it arrive in Amsterdam?

At quarter past four. Here's your ticket.

⁶_____ a lot.

The bus leaves ⁷_____ gate twenty-four.

B Listen again and say the sentences at the same time.

C Work in pairs and take turns. Practise the conversation.

▶ page 128 **LANGUAGEBANK**

LEARN TO check numbers

4A ▶ 6.7 Listen and underline the stressed syllable in the numbers.

B: The bus leaves from gate twenty-four.

A: Sorry? Gate thirty-four?

B: No, gate twenty-four.

A: Thanks a lot.

B Listen again and repeat.

speakout TIP

Use stress to check and correct numbers. *Sorry, fifty-five? No, fifty-nine.*

C Work in pairs and take turns. Practise the conversations.

1 A: That's €250.
   B: Sorry? 240?
   A: No, 250.

2 B: It's bus number 72.
   A: Sorry? 72?
   B: Yes, that's right. 72.

3 A: The train leaves at 5 o'clock.
   B: Sorry? 9 o'clock?
   A: No, 5 o'clock.

5A Write down two prices, two train times and two bus numbers. Don't show your partner.

B Work in pairs and take turns. Student A: read your numbers fast. Student B: repeat the numbers to check.

A: Two dollars and forty cents.

B: Sorry? Ten dollars and forty cents?

A: No, two dollars and forty cents.

SPEAKING

6A Work in pairs. Student A: look at the information below. Student B: turn to page 150.

Student A: you are at a bus station in Amsterdam. You want to buy a ticket. Ask Student B questions to complete the table.

ticket	a single to Brussels
price	
time of next bus	
gate	
arrival time	

B Change roles. Student A: you work in a ticket office in the central train station in Amsterdam. Look at the information and answer Student B's questions.

ticket	a return to Paris
price	€174
time of next train	8.30a.m.
platform	6
arrival time	12.45p.m.

6.4 RUSH HOUR

DVD PREVIEW

1A What do you know about India? Look at the words in the box below. Cross out the one which is <u>not</u> in or from India.

1 Karachi, Mumbai, Delhi
2 Mahatma Gandhi, Omar Sharif, Mother Teresa
3 Bollywood, coffee, yoga
4 River Ganges, Taj Mahal, Machu Picchu
5 daal, nan, tempura

B Read the programme information and look at the photos. How do people go to work and school in India?

BBC Visions Of India: Rush Hour

Each programme in the BBC's *Visions Of India* shows a different side of this country of one billion people. This programme looks at how millions of working Indians travel to work and school every day.

DVD VIEW

2A Watch the DVD to check your ideas in Exercise 1B.

B Complete the sentences with the adjectives in the box below.

> ~~popular~~ crowded slow dangerous noisy expensive

1 A lot of people like it. It's _popular_.
2 It isn't quiet. It's _____.
3 It costs a lot. It's _____.
4 It isn't safe. It's _____.
5 It has a lot of people. It's _____.
6 It isn't fast. It's _____.

C Watch the DVD again and underline the adjectives you hear for each type of transport.

1 trains – <u>crowded</u>, popular, noisy
2 bikes – dangerous, fast, slow
3 motorbikes – fast, noisy, dangerous
4 tuk-tuks – popular, fast, noisy
5 taxis – fast, safe, expensive

speakout a travel survey

3A Work in pairs and discuss. How do people in your country travel in cities and in the countryside?

B ▶ 6.8 Listen to a student describe travel in his country and complete the table.

in a big city	in the countryside
I	I
2	2
3	3

C Listen again and tick the key phrases you hear.

keyphrases

I live in (London) but I'm from (the countryside).

There's a good public transport system.

(A lot of/Some people) use (the underground/buses).

Some people go to work by (bus/bike).

The best way to travel is by (car/underground).

People also go by (bus).

In (my village/the city), I go everywhere by (car/bike).

4A Work with a new partner and talk about the different ways people travel in your country. Use the key phrases to help.

B Work in groups and tell other students.

writeback a travel forum entry

5A A travel website asks people to write about transport in their town/city. Read the forum entry. How does the writer usually travel?

I live in Kobe, Japan and I work in Osaka. I think the best way to travel is by train. I go by the JR train line every morning. There are sometimes ten trains every hour. It's about thirty minutes from Kobe to Osaka. I have a monthly pass but I think a single ticket is about 500 yen.

In Kobe, people travel by car, but there's a good public transport system, so a lot of people use buses and the underground. A one-day tourist pass is 1,000 yen. I live near the centre so I usually walk everywhere. Kobe is a small city, and it's a good city for walkers.

B Write about transport in your town/city or a town/city you know for the travel website. Write 80–100 words.

PLACES

1A Add the vowels to the places.

1 i n t e rn e t c a f é
2 r__st__ __r__nt
3 ph__rm__cy
4 n__ws__g__nt's
5 p__yph__n__
6 c__sh m__ch__n__
7 h__t__l
8 sn__ck b__r

B Work in pairs. Write a thing/ activity connected to the places above.

internet café – email

C Work in groups. Student A: say one thing/activity. Other students: guess the place.
A: *Email.*
B: *Internet café.*
A: *That's right.*

THERE IS/ARE

2A Complete the questions asked in a hotel with *Is there* or *Are there*.

1 __Is there__ a swimming pool?
2 _____ a restaurant in the hotel?
3 _____ two beds in my room?
4 _____ a guided tour of the city tomorrow?
5 _____ any cash machines near the hotel?
6 _____ any other hotels near here?

B Match answers a)–f) with the questions above.

a) No, _____, but the city isn't very interesting.
b) Yes, _____ but they're all full.
c) Yes, _____, but the water is very cold.
d) Yes, _____, but it's closed now. It's open for dinner.
e) No, _____. _____ only one bed.
f) No, _____, but _____ one <u>in</u> the hotel.

C Complete the answers above with *there is/ 's*, *there are*, *there isn't* or *there aren't*.

TRANSPORT

3A Circle eight transport words.

Q	P	B	H	I	U	M
B	U	S	F	H	N	O
I	A	S	N	B	D	T
K	P	L	A	N	E	O
E	E	G	J	T	R	R
K	Z	Y	G	Z	G	B
E	O	K	R	E	R	I
T	R	A	E	N	O	K
A	T	R	C	U	U	E
X	T	R	A	I	N	H
I	W	S	R	S	D	K

B Work in groups and take turns. Student A: draw a picture of one of the things in Exercise 3A. Other students: guess what it is.

A/AN, SOME, A LOT OF, NOT ANY

4A Find and correct the mistakes in the sentences.

In this book:

1 A lot ⌃*of* pages don't have photos.
2 Some page have six photos.
3 There's an Spanish word on page 6.
4 There's blue glove on page 32.

B Work in pairs. Which sentences above are true? Change the others to make them true.

C Work in pairs. Write four more sentences about the book, but only one true sentence. Use *a/an*, *some*, *a lot of* and *not any*.

D Work in groups and take turns to read out your sentences. Which sentences are true?

TRAVEL

5 Complete the words.

1 You buy a ticket at the ticket of__ __ __ __ __.
2 The people on the bus are pas__ __ __ __ __ __ __ __ __s.
3 The bus leaves from a ga__ __ __.
4 A ticket from A to B is a si__ __ __ __ __ __.
5 A ticket from A to B to A is a re__ __ __ __ __ __.
6 A ticket for four weeks is a mo__ __ __ __ __ __ __ pass.

BUYING A TICKET

6A Complete the conversation.

A: ¹single / Lisbon, / please.
A single to Lisbon, please.
B: For when?
A: ²I / want / go / tomorrow morning.
B: OK. That's €39.
A: ³What time / first bus?
B: There's one at 10.40.
A: ⁴What time / it / arrive / Lisbon?
B: At 12.15.
A: ⁵Where / it / leave / from?
B: It leaves from gate 34.
A: ⁶Thanks / lot.

B Work in pairs and practise the conversation.

BBC VIDEO PODCAST

Watch people talking about how they get to school or work on ActiveBook or on the website.

Authentic BBC interviews

www.pearsonELT.com/speakout

READING AND GRAMMAR

1A Work in pairs and discuss the questions.

When you have a problem, do you usually:

• talk to people in your family about it?

• talk to one or two friends about it?

• phone or email a lot of people about it?

• look on the internet?

• write to a website about it?

• think about it alone?

B Read the text. Match answers a)–c) with problems 1–3.

QUICKANSWERS

You tell us your problem and other people answer

1 My problem is I'm always tired. I work in a snack bar from seven in the morning to six in the evening. I drink a lot of cups of coffee at work because I'm tired. I never have breakfast but I usually have a sandwich and a cake for lunch. I don't often go out in the evenings because I'm tired. **Jon**

2 My husband does nothing in the house. I often get home after work and there isn't any food in the flat so I always buy food and cook. He says he isn't hungry and he doesn't want a big dinner. He wants to sit down and watch TV all evening. I think it's important to have dinner together and talk. **Layla**

3 There are a lot of beautiful places in the world but I never see them. My problem is I don't like travelling by plane, train, boat or car so I never go on holiday. **Rob**

a) How about bikes? Try a cycling holiday.

b) It's important to sit down and talk.

c) Change your job!

C Work in pairs and read the text again. Write your answers to the three people.

1 After work, go to the gym and do exercise. It's good for you.

2A Put the words in the correct order to make questions about the three people.

1a) Jon / breakfast / Does / have?
   Does Jon have breakfast?

 b) evenings / go / in / Does / he / out / the?

2a) buy / the / Layla / food / Does?

 b) her / home / husband / What / at / does / do?

3a) there / planes / Is / problem / a / with?

 b) does / on / holiday / Rob / When / go?

B Match answers 1–6 with questions 1a)–3b) above.

1 No, not often. *1b*

2 Yes, she does.

3 Yes, there is.

4 No, he doesn't but he has lunch.

5 Nothing.

6 He doesn't. He always stays at home.

LISTENING AND GRAMMAR

3A ▶ R3.1 Listen and match conversations 1–5 with the places in the box. Where is each person? You do **not** need to use one of the places.

snack bar *1* pharmacy cash machine newsagent's payphone internet café

B Listen again and underline the correct alternative.

	What's the problem?	What happens?
1	The coffee isn't *hot/good*.	She gets *a tea/another coffee*.
2	The shop *never has/doesn't have* the New York Times.	He *buys/doesn't buy* another paper.
3	The cash machine *doesn't have money/is broken*.	*She/Salvatore* has some money.
4	Computer number *three/five* is broken.	He *goes to another computer/leaves*.
5	He's *cold/ill*.	He *buys/doesn't buy* something for it.

SPEAKING

4A Work in pairs. Look at audio script Review 3.1 on page 158. Choose one of the conversations and practise it.

B Write six to eight keywords to help you remember the conversations.

A:
Excuse
problem, coffee, cold

B:
Yeah
Sorry, let me …

C Role-play the situation. Use the keywords to help.

5A Work in pairs. Choose a place from Exercise 3A and a problem. Answer the questions.
1 Where are you?
2 Who are you?
3 What's the problem?

1 newsagent's
2 customer and shop assistant
3 I want a newspaper and I only have a 20-euro note

B Role-play a conversation between the two people in the place.

C Work in groups and take turns to listen to other students' conversations. What place are they in?

SOUNDS: /ð/ AND /θ/

6A ▶ R3.2 Listen to the sounds and the words. Then listen and repeat.

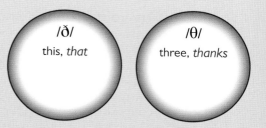

/ð/	/θ/
this	three

B ▶ R3.3 Listen and put the words in the box in the correct group. Then listen and repeat.

~~thanks~~ ~~that~~ monthly thirsty father
with think these together thirteen

/ð/
this, *that*

/θ/
three, *thanks*

7A ▶ R3.4 Listen and circle the correct pronunciation.
1 together   a)   b)
2 think   a)   b)
3 these   a)   b)
4 thirsty   a)   b)
5 father   a)   b)
6 the   a)   b)
7 thank you   a)   b)
8 three   a)   b)
9 brother   a)   b)
10 month   a)   b)

B Work in pairs and take turns. Say the sentences slowly.
1 These three brothers are dirty and thirsty.
2 They say thanks for the time together.
3 There are three big airports in South Africa.

C Work in pairs. Say each sentence at the same time. Speak fast.

UNIT 7

SPEAKING
- ❯ Find out where people were in the past
- ❯ Talk about the past
- ❯ Give your opinion
- ❯ Do a history quiz

LISTENING
- ❯ Listen to people talk about New Year 2000
- ❯ Listen to people give opinions
- ❯ Watch a BBC programme about the Chilean miners

READING
- ❯ Read about amazing records

WRITING
- ❯ Improve your punctuation
- ❯ Write a history quiz

BBC CONTENT
- ▯ Video podcast: Where were you on your last birthday?
- ◉ DVD: The Chilean Miners

UNIT **7**

past

▶ **Where were you?** p74

▶ **Record breakers** p76

▶ **How was it?** p78

▶ **The Chilean Miners** p80

7.1 WHERE WERE YOU?

GRAMMAR | past simple: *was/were* — VOCABULARY | dates — HOW TO | talk about where you were

LISTENING

1A Work in pairs and look at the photos. What time of year is it? What do you usually do at this time of year?

B 7.1 Listen to people talk about New Year 2000. Match the speakers and the places.

Speaker 1	at a concert
Speaker 2	at home
Speaker 3	at work
Speaker 4	in hospital
Speaker 5	on a beach

C Listen again and answer the questions.

Who talks about:

a) family? *1*
b) friends?
c) fireworks? *1*
d) music?
e) the sunrise?
f) a party? *1*
g) money?
h) hospital?

GRAMMAR past simple: *was/were*

2A Underline the correct alternative.

1 I *am/was* at home. There *is/was* a family party.
2 We *are/were* in Miami.
3 We *aren't/weren't* alone.
4 *Was/Were* the party for me?

B Complete the table with *was*, *wasn't*, *were* or *weren't*.

I He/She/It	*was* ______	at home. in Beijing. tired.
You/We/They	______ weren't	

Was ______	he you	here? in class?
Yes,	he we	______. were.
No,	he we	______. ______.

3A 7.2 Listen to the sentences and mark the stress.

1 I was at home.
2 We were tired.
3 She was in class.
4 They were here.

B Listen again to the pronunciation of *was* /wəz/ and *were* /wə/. Then listen and repeat.

page 130 LANGUAGEBANK

PRACTICE

4A Underline the correct alternative.

1 Where *was/were* you at New Year 2000? *Was/Were* you alone or with friends?
2 *Was/Were* you and your friends at a concert last New Year?
3 *Was/Were* there a party on your last birthday? Where *was/were* it? *Was/Were* your friends there?
4 What *was/were* the last public holiday in your country? Where *was/were* you? Who *was/were* there?

B Complete the answers to questions 1–4 above. Use *was*, *wasn't*, *were* or *weren't*.

a) I *was* on a mountain in Slovakia. I ______ alone – there ______ about twenty of my friends with me.
b) No, we ______. We ______ at a party on a boat on the River Thames.
c) Yes, there ______, but it ______ a big party because my flat's very small.
d) Our last public holiday ______ Thanksgiving. We ______ at my brother's house. My parents ______ there because they ______ on holiday in Jamaica.

C Work in pairs and take turns. Ask and answer questions 1–4 from Exercise 4A.

A: *Where were you at New Year 2000?*
B: *I was in Peru.*
A: *Were you alone?*
B: *No, I wasn't. I was at a party with people from work. What about you?*

speakout TIP

Three questions are very useful to help you to have a good conversation: *What about you? How about you? And you?* Write these questions in your phrase book.

VOCABULARY dates

5A Number the months in order.

September	____	June	____	February	____
March	____	December	____	October	____
January	*1*	July	____	August	____
May	____	November	____	April	____

B ▶ 7.3 Listen and check. Then listen and repeat.

C Work in pairs and take turns. Student A: say a month. Student B: say the next month.

A: May   *B: June*

6A Match the numbers with the words.

1st	fifth
2nd	second
3rd	twentieth
4th	fourth
5th	twenty-first
15th	third
20th	first
21st	fifteenth

B ▶ 7.4 Listen and number the dates in the order you hear them.

October 15th	___	August 8th	___
December 1st	*1*	September 21st	___
April 16th	___	March 25th	___

C Listen again and repeat the dates.
*December **the** first*

7A Work in pairs. Write three important dates in your life or in your country. Student A: say the dates. Student B: write the dates down.

B Ask each other about the dates.
B: Why is March the nineteenth important?
A: It's my birthday.

▶ page 145 **PHOTOBANK**

SPEAKING

8A It is Monday at 9a.m. Number the past time phrases in order.

a) last Friday ___
b) last month ___
c) yesterday evening *1*
d) this time last year *5*
e) on Saturday afternoon ___

B Work in pairs and take turns. Ask about the times in Exercise 8A.
A: Where were you last Friday?
B: I was at home.

WRITING punctuation review

9A Match 1–5 with punctuation marks a)–e).

1	comma *e)*		a)	!
2	full stop		b)	.
3	exclamation mark		c)	?
4	question mark		d)	A
5	capital letter		e)	,

B Read the email. Where's Jane? Where's Paola?

Date	28/7/2012

Hi paola [1]___
How are you [2]___ I'm fine and I'm in ✳✳✳✳✳
with matt [3]___ We're on holiday here [4]___
Yesterday we were at the opening of the olympic
games [5]___ Was it on television
in italy [6]___ It was great [7]___ There was
dancing [8]___ singing and fantastic fireworks [9]___
Here's a photo [10]___ Write soon [11]___
Best wishes [12]___
jane

C Complete the email with punctuation marks and change six letters to capital letters.

10A Write an email from a special place and on a special day. Write three things about the place but don't write the name of the place.

B Work in groups and read other students' emails. Guess the place.

VOCABULARY actions

1A ▶ 7.5 Listen and write the number next to the action you hear.

laugh ___	arrive ___
start _1_	dance ___
walk ___	cry ___
play tennis ___	talk ___
move home ___	wait ___

B Work in pairs. Student A: act one of the verbs. Student B: say the verb.

READING

2A Look at the photos. Which actions from Exercise 1A can you see? Where are the people?

B Read the article and write the headlines in the correct place.

> **Man talks for six days**
> *Dance marathon*
> Non-stop tennis match
> **Woman walks round world**

C Read the article again and write the names.
1 He laughed. *Mike Ritof*
2 She moved twenty-four times.
3 He played tennis with Daniel.
4 People listened to him.
5 She cried.

D Read the article again and correct the mistakes in the notes below.

> dancing: 5,512 hours and
> 44 minutes
>
> walking: 32,000 metres
>
> talking: 212 hours
>
> playing tennis: 32 hours,
> 12 minutes, 6 seconds

1 _____

Ffyona Campbell walked around the world – that's 32,000 kilometres in eleven years. In Africa, she started in Cape Town in 1991 and arrived in Tangiers in 1993. Why did she walk so much? Well, maybe it was because of her childhood: she moved home twenty-four times before she was sixteen!

2 _____

Mike Ritof and Edith Boudreaux started dancing at the Merry Garden Ballroom, Chicago on August 29th 1930, and danced for 5,152 hours and 48 minutes (with short breaks). When they finally stopped on April 1st 1931, she cried and he laughed.

3 _____

Carlo Santelli and Daniel Burns played tennis for 38 hours, two minutes and nine seconds on May 10th 2010 in Clifton, New Jersey, USA. We didn't ask them about the winner – they were so happy about getting the world record!

4 _____

Errol Muzawazi of Zimbabwe talked about democracy for 121 hours from December 9th to 14th 2009. One audience member said, 'I listened for thirteen hours and waited for him to stop, but he didn't!'

GRAMMAR past simple: regular verbs

3A Read the article again and find the past form of the verbs below.

1	start *started*	5	laugh	9	talk
2	dance	6	walk	10	listen
3	move	7	arrive	11	wait
4	cry	8	stop	12	play

B Complete the table.

Rule: to make the past simple with regular verbs:

	spelling	examples
most verbs	add _____	*started, laughed*
verbs ending in -e	add _____	_____
verbs ending in consonant + -y	change to _____	_____
most verbs ending in consonant + vowel + consonant	double the final letter, then add _____	_____

C Look at the sentence and complete the rule.

We didn't ask them about the winner …

Rule:
Use _____ + verb to make the negative of the past simple.

4A ▶ 7.6 Listen to the pronunciation of the verbs and write them in the correct place.

/t/ *danced*
/d/ *moved*
/ɪd/ *started*

B ▶ 7.7 Listen and check. Then listen and repeat.

▐▶ page 130 **LANGUAGEBANK**

PRACTICE

5A Complete the sentences with the past form of the verbs in brackets.

1 He _____ (live) here when he was a boy, **but** then he _____ (move) to the countryside.
2 We _____ (wait) for hours, **but** the bus _____ (not arrive).
3 My friend _____ (cook) dinner last night **and** I really _____ (like) it.
4 I usually drive, but yesterday I _____ (walk) **because** they _____ (close) the road.
5 The teacher _____ (ask) me a question, **but** I _____ (not understand).
6 I _____ (watch) a very sad film last night **and** I _____ (cry) the whole time.

B Work in pairs and take turns. Student A: close your book. Student B: read the first part of the sentences. Stop after the word in bold. Student A: try to remember the end of the sentence.
*B: He lived here when he was a boy, **but** …*
A: … then he moved to the countryside.

SPEAKING

6A Make three true sentences and three false sentences.

* Write the name of a friend or student here.

B Work in groups and take turns. Student A: read one of your sentences. Other students: say if it's true or false.
A: Simon danced with Lena last weekend.
B: False.
A: That's right. He didn't dance with Lena. He danced with Bea.

FUNCTION | giving opinions   **VOCABULARY** | adjectives   **LEARN TO** | show feelings

VOCABULARY adjectives

1A Work in pairs. Complete the table with the adjectives in the box.

> all right   terrible   delicious   OK
> awful   great   fantastic   not very good
> boring   interesting

+	delicious
–	terrible
+/–	all right

B Work in pairs and write:

1 ++ next to three adjectives that mean <u>very</u> good.

2 – – next to two adjectives that mean <u>very</u> bad.

3 F next to an adjective that is <u>only</u> for food.

C ▶ 7.8 Listen and underline the stress in the adjectives. Then listen and repeat.

all <u>right</u>

2A Write the name of a person, place or thing for each adjective in Exercise 1A.

fantastic – Daniel Craig
boring – golf
all right – my town

B Work in pairs and take turns. Student A: say a person, place or thing on your list. Student B: guess Student A's adjective.

A: Golf.
B: Great?
A: No.
B: Boring?
A: Yes!

⫸ page 145 **PHOTOBANK**

FUNCTION giving opinions

3A ▶ 7.9 Listen to four conversations. Are the conversations about a concert (C), a film (F), a party (P) or a restaurant meal (R)? Write the letter.

1 _F_   2 ____   3 ____   4 ____

B Listen again. Match phrases 1–8 with a)–h).

1	This is good.	a)	steak
2	It was very good.	b)	chicken
3	It's terrible.	c)	singer
4	It was boring	d)	ice cream
5	It wasn't very good.	e)	Warren's party
6	She was great.	f)	concert
7	Fantastic.	g)	film
8	Delicious.	h)	Alan's party

4A ▶ 7.10 Put the words in order to make questions and opinions. Then listen and check.

1 A: was / your / How / steak?
   B: Delicious, / right / just

2 A: your / was / chicken / How?
   B: good / It / very / wasn't

3 A: How / concert / the / was?
   B: fantastic / band / was / The

4 A: party / was / the / How?
   B: boring / It / was

B Underline two stressed words in each question or phrase above.

C Listen and check. Then listen and repeat.

D Work in pairs and practise the conversations.

⫸ page 130 **LANGUAGEBANK**

LEARN TO show feelings

5A ▶ **7.10** Listen to the phrases again. Is speaker B's voice high (H) or low (L)?

1 ___   2 ___   3 ___   4 ___

> **speakout TIP**
>
> When you give an opinion, use high intonation for a positive feeling (*Beautiful!*), and flat or low intonation for a negative feeling (*Terrible!*)

B Work in pairs and take turns. Ask and answer questions using the words in the circles. Use high or low intonation in your answers.

Circle 1:
- the film?
- the concert?
- the party?
- your holiday?
- the food?
- your weekend?

Circle 2:
- great
- fantastic
- delicious
- not very good
- terrible
- awful
- very nice
- boring

A: How was your holiday?
B: It wasn't very good.

SPEAKING

6A Complete the conversation.

Student A	Student B
Where / you / last night?	
	I / Kelly's party.
How / it?	
	It / not very good. I / not like / it.
Why not?	
	The people / boring / the music / awful. Where / you?
I / cinema.	
	Which film / it?
(name of film)	
	How / it?
It / great! I / really / like / it.	
	Who / in it?
(name of actor or actress). He/She / very good.	

B Work in pairs and take turns. Role-play the conversation.

C Change the conversation to talk about a restaurant and a concert.
A: Where were you last night?
B: I was at the new Chinese restaurant.
A: Oh, how was it?

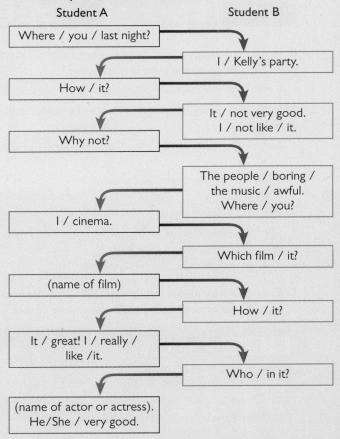

DVD PREVIEW

1A Work in pairs and match the words in the box with pictures A–H.

> drill *A*   miner   tunnel   microphone   note
> underground   surface   accident

B What do you know about the Chilean miners' story? Work in pairs and underline the correct alternative.

1 It was in *2008/2009/2010*.

2 There was *an accident/a lot of rain/a plane crash* at the mine.

3 There were *23/33/43* miners underground.

4 For the first *3/7/17* days, many people were sure the men were dead.

5 Then *a note/a text message/an email* arrived from the men. They were OK!

6 Workers drilled a tunnel to the miners for 7 *days/weeks/months*.

7 The first miner arrived at the surface in *the morning/in the afternoon/at night*.

8 The last man out was the *president/chef/boss*.

C Read the programme information. Which sentences in Exercise 1B does it give information about? Were your answers correct?

▶ DVD VIEW

2A Watch the DVD to check your answers to the other sentences in Exercise 1B.

B Complete sentences 1–6 with words from the box below.

> ~~seven~~   days   worked   families
> well   travelled   minutes   rescue

1 Thirty-three miners were underground, _seven_ hundred metres underground.

2 'We are _____ in the shelter, the 33'.

3 The miners _____ to keep healthy and positive.

4 The miners' _____ watched and waited.

5 The tunnel was finished. The _____ started.

6 It was eighteen _____ from the mine to the surface.

7 One by one the miners _____ to the surface.

8 After sixty-nine _____, the miners were free.

C Watch the DVD again to check your answers.

BBC The Chilean Miners' Rescue

In 2010 there was an accident at a mine near Copiapó, Chile. 33 miners were underground at the time. Were they dead or alive? For 17 days, their families and friends waited. Then, on Day 17, a note arrived from the mine: it was from the men. They were OK. Workers drilled down to the miners for many weeks. People around the world watched and waited. Finally, after 69 days, one by one, the miners travelled to the surface. They were free! Watch their story on tonight's *Newsround*.

speakout a history quiz

3A Work in pairs. Put the news events on the timeline.

a) Michael Jackson died
b) Asian tsunami
c) Google started
d) Chernobyl nuclear accident

1986   1991   1996   2000   2004   2009

B ▶ 7.11 Listen to two people do the task and check your answers.

C Listen again and tick the key phrases you hear.

keyphrases

Which was first?

I think (Chernobyl / the Asian tsunami) was (first / next).

Yes, I agree.

I don't know./I'm not sure.

No, (Google) was before (the Asian tsunami).

No, (it) was after (the Asian tsunami).

Which date?

It was before my time.

I remember it well.

Let's check the answers.

We were (right/wrong) about (three answers/ Google.)

D Work in groups. Look at page 151 and do the quiz. Use the key phrases to help.

writeback a history quiz

4A Read and answer three questions from a quiz.

1 When were the first modern Olympic Games?
a) 776
b) 1896
c) 1906
2 Which US president's father was also president?
a) John Kennedy
b) George W. Bush
c) Barack Obama
3 Why was Evita famous?
a) she was a politician
b) she was a singer
c) she was a sportswoman

See answers at the bottom of the page.

B Work in pairs and write three more questions. Use the prompts to help.

| When … ? | Where … ? | Who … ? |
| What … ? |
| Which (king, queen, president, country, etc.) … ? | Why … ? |

C Work with a new partner and take turns. Ask and answer your questions.

Answers: 1b), 2b), 3a)

PAST SIMPLE: WAS/WERE

1A Write the questions for 1–8.

Find someone who ...

1 was very happy yesterday.
   Were you very happy yesterday?
2 was tired this morning.
3 was in the town/city centre at the weekend.
4 was here in the last class.
5 was in a café before class.
6 was on a train at eight o'clock this morning.
7 was late for something yesterday.
8 was ill yesterday.

B Work in groups and ask the questions. If a student says *yes*, write his/her name.

A: Were you very happy yesterday?
B: Yes, I was. It was my birthday.

DATES

2A Write today's date. _____

B Write the dates for the time phrases below.

1 yesterday _____
2 last year _____
3 last month _____
4 last Saturday _____
5 on Tuesday _____
6 last night _____

C Work in pairs. Student A: say a time phrase from Exercise 2B. Student B: say the date.

D Write a different date and repeat Exercise 2C.

Friday June 3rd 2011

A: Yesterday.
B: Thursday June 2nd 2011.
A: Last year.
B: 2010.

ACTIONS

3A Put the letters in the correct order to make actions.

1 twia *wait*   5 gluha
2 ktla   6 ryc
3 nacde   7 ratts
4 veria   8 klaw

B Complete the sentences with one of the verbs above.

1 People say that I *laugh* and smile a lot.
2 I never _____ late for the lesson.
3 My day _____ at six o'clock in the morning.
4 The teacher sometimes _____ too fast.
5 Sometimes I _____ to work, sometimes I drive.
6 At a party, I _____ if the music is good.
7 I don't _____ when I'm sad.
8 I never _____ when someone is late for a meeting.

C Work in pairs. Which of the sentences in Exercise 3B are true for you? Change the other sentences to make them true.

PAST SIMPLE: REGULAR VERBS

4A Change the verbs to the past form.

1 watch*ed* a film on a plane
2 wait____ for a bus
3 phone____ someone in your family
4 ask____ a question on the internet
5 laugh____ a lot
6 play____ with a child
7 cry____ at a film
8 study____ English grammar
9 stop____ someone on the street
10 dance____ at a club

B Work in pairs and take turns. Ask and answer questions with the phrases above. Start your question: *When was the last time you ... ?*

A: When was the last time you watched a film on a plane?
B: Last year. I was on a plane from Madrid to Berlin. The film was ...

ADJECTIVES

5A Add the vowels to the adjectives.

1 t__rr__bl__
2 d__l__c_____s
3 __nt__r__st__ng
4 __wf__l
5 f__nt__st__c
6 b__r__ng
7 gr____t
8 __ll r__ght
9 n__t v__ry g____d
10 __K

B Work in pairs and make short conversations. Use the adjectives above and words in the box.

> the film   the food   the match
> the concert   the lesson

A: The concert was terrible!
B: Yes, it was awful.

GIVING OPINIONS

6A Put the sentences in order to make a conversation.

A: Why not?
A: It was great.
A: How was the restaurant? *1*
A: She thinks it was all right.

B: How was it for Anne?
B: It wasn't very good. *2*
B: Because the food was terrible. And the film?

B Work in pairs and practise the conversation.

UNIT
8

SPEAKING
> › Talk about first meetings
> › Ask and answer about a good holiday
> › Give directions in a supermarket
> › Tell a bad holiday story

LISTENING
> › Listen to a radio programme about holidays
> › Watch a BBC comedy about tourists in Spain

READING
> › Read about how people met their friends

WRITING
> › Use linkers: *so* and *because*
> › Write a bad holiday story

BBC content
> ▣ Video podcast: Where did you go on holiday last year?
> ◉ DVD: Little Britain

places

▶ Nice place to meet p84

▶ Good and bad p86

▶ Where's the fruit? p88

▶ Guided Tour p90

READING

1A Work in pairs. Where do people usually meet friends for the first time?

B Read the text. Which story is really unusual?

C Underline the mistake in each sentence. Try to remember the correct information from the text.

1 The bridge was in Northern Scotland.

2 Cynthia and Anne were on the bridge for an hour.

3 The taxi driver worked in London.

4 Darnell worked at a shop.

5 Jon was in a train accident.

6 Jon was in hospital for a month.

7 Someone took Alison's passport.

8 The waitress said, 'Do you need money?'

D Read the text again and check your answers.

GRAMMAR past simple: irregular verbs

2A Write the past forms of the verbs. Use the text in Exercise 1B to help. Check the meaning of any new words.

1	meet	_met_	6	break	_____
2	come	_____	7	go	_____
3	take	_____	8	have	_____
4	think	_____	9	sit	_____
5	become	_____	10	say	_____

B ▶ 8.1 Listen and check. Then listen and repeat.

C Underline the correct alternative to make the negative. Use the text to help.

I *didn't have/didn't had* any money.

> ❝ **speakout** TIP
>
> When you learn a new verb, check your dictionary and write the past form in your phrase book, e.g. *go – went*. For regular verbs, write 'reg', e.g. *play* (reg). Do this with these verbs: *drive, know, stay, see, give.*

▥➡ page 132 **LANGUAGEBANK**

Unusual Stories

Win a holiday for two. Tell us where you met your best friend.

On a rope bridge in Northern Ireland! I walked from one side, and another woman, Anne, walked from the other side. We met in the centre, and we were both very scared. We were there for half an hour. Finally, a guide came and helped us. After that half-hour together we were friends for life. **Cynthia**

In my taxi in New York City. I was a taxi driver in New York in the 1990s and I worked at night. Darnell worked at a club, and I took him home at 4a.m. every night. I thought he was a really nice person. We talked a lot and became great friends. **Oliver**

In hospital in China. I was in a car accident and broke my leg. I went to hospital and was there for a week. There was a Chinese guy in my room, Li. We had a lot of time to talk and became great friends. **Jon**

In a café in Argentina. I was on holiday and someone took my money. I sat down in a café. I didn't have any money but I was very hungry. The waitress came to my table and said, 'Hi, I'm Claudia. Do you need help?' We were instant best friends! **Alison**

PRACTICE

3A Read the stories. Who are the people?

1

In the 1990s, [1]I ____was____ (be) a singer at a club in New York. The first night there I [2]_____ (finish) work at 4a.m. and I [3]_____ (not want) to walk home so I [4]_____ (stop) Oliver's taxi and he [5]_____ (drive) me home. I [6]_____ (think) he was a great guy and later we [7]_____ (become) good friends.

2

In 2008, I [8]_____ (work) as a waitress at a café. One day I was at work and I [9]_____ (see) a woman alone and very unhappy. I [10]_____ (go) over to her and [11]_____ (say), 'Hi, do you need help?' She [12]_____ (not have) any money and she [13]_____ (not know) anyone in the city. I [14]_____ (give) her some money and food. Now she's one of my best friends.

B Complete the stories with the past forms of the verbs in brackets.

C Work in pairs. Student A: change three things in story 1. Student B: change three things in story 2.

D Work in pairs and take turns. Student A: read your story. Student B: listen to Student A and stop the story when you hear something different.

A: I was a singer at a club in London.

B: Stop! No, you were a singer at a club in New York.

VOCABULARY prepositions of place

4A Underline the correct alternative.

1 We were *at / in / on* a bridge.
2 We met *at / in / on* New York.
3 I was *at / in / on* work.

B Complete the word webs with *in*, *on* or *at*.

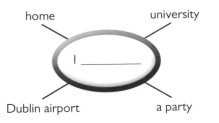

home   university

1 _____

Dublin airport   a party

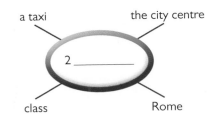

a taxi   the city centre

2 _____

class   Rome

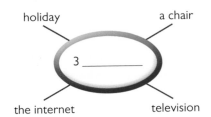

holiday   a chair

3 _____

the internet   television

5A Complete the sentences with *in*, *on* or *at*.

1 I met my best friend *at* university.
2 I met one of my friends the internet.
3 I went holiday with a friend last year.
4 I met a great friend my English class last month.
5 I was a friend's party on Saturday.
6 I had lunch with a friend the city centre yesterday.

B Tick the sentences that are true for you. Change the other sentences to make them true for you.

▸ page 146 **PHOTOBANK**

SPEAKING

6A Write the name of three friends on the timeline. Write the year and place you met.

Viki

2005
University   Now

B Work in groups and take turns. Show your timeline and talk about your friends.

Viki is a good friend. We met in 2005 at university. We were students.

VOCABULARY holiday activities

1A Match verbs 1–4 with a)–d) and verbs 5–8 with e)–h).

1	see	a) the local water
2	eat	b) ill
3	drink	c) old buildings
4	be	d) the local food
5	go	e) English
6	meet	f) a good time
7	speak	g) camping
8	have	h) the local people

B Work in pairs. Which activities above are in the pictures?

C Work in pairs and take turns. Student A: say the ending. Student B: say the activity.

A: old buildings
B: see old buildings

D Work in pairs and take turns to ask and answer. Which activities do you do when you're on holiday?

A: On holiday, do you drink the local water?
B: Yes, I do, but I sometimes drink mineral water. How about you?

LISTENING

2A Work alone. Number the holidays in order (1–5). 1 = My favourite type of holiday, 5 = I don't like this type of holiday.

a) a camping holiday with your family ____
b) a holiday in Sydney, Australia ____
c) a weekend in Paris, France ____
d) two months in China alone ____
e) a walking holiday in Peru with a friend ____

B Work in pairs and compare your answers.

A: For number one, I put a weekend in Paris.
B: Why?
A: I like France and Paris is beautiful. What about you?

3A ▶ 8.2 Listen to a radio programme about good and bad holidays. Write good (G) or bad (B) next to the holidays in Exercise 2A.

B Underline the correct information. Then listen again and check your ideas.

1 He went camping in *Canada*/ *Cambodia*.
2 They didn't have *tea*/ *television*.
3 He lost his *passport*/ *girlfriend*.
4 He had some bad *food*/ *water*.
5 She *got*/ *didn't get* to Paris.
6 She ate *lunch*/ *dinner* on the train.
7 She met *English*/ *Chinese* people.
8 She *spoke*/ *didn't speak* Chinese.

GRAMMAR past simple: questions

4A ▶ 8.3 Listen and complete the table.

Questions and short answers							
—	you	like	it?	Yes,	I	___.
		speak	English?	No,		___.
Wh- questions						
Where	—	you	go?			
What			do?			

B Listen to the questions and short answers. Then listen and repeat.

Did‿you ...?

➠ page 132 **LANGUAGEBANK**

PRACTICE

5A Put the words in the correct order to make questions.

1 on / go / you / holiday / last / Did / summer?
2 have / weather / on / good / you / Did / holiday?
3 eat / a / restaurant / you / in / Did / yesterday?
4 you / your / last / friends / night / Did / meet?
5 English / you / yesterday / speak / Did?
6 breakfast / this / have / Did / morning / you?

B Complete the answers.

1 (+ I / to Greece) *Yes, I did. I went to Greece.*
2 (+ we / it / very hot)
3 (– I / at home)
4 (– I / last weekend)
5 (+ I / with my teacher)
6 (+ we / toast and coffee)

C Work in pairs and take turns. Ask the questions in Exercise 5A and answer about you.

A: Did you go on holiday last summer?
B: Yes, I did. I went to Bulgaria, to the Black Sea.

➠ page 146 **PHOTOBANK**

SPEAKING

6A Work alone. Write notes to answer the questions about a good holiday.

1 Where and when did you go?
2 Did you go alone or with friends or family?
3 How did you travel?
4 Where did you stay?
5 Did you have good weather?
6 What did you do?
7 Why did you like it?

1 Colombia – in 2010 – four weeks

B Work in groups and take turns. Student A: talk about your holiday. Other students: ask questions.

WRITING so and because

7A Match sentences 1–3 with a)–c).

Holiday mistakes

1 In Denmark, we went camping because the hotels were expensive.
2 In Hong Kong, I thought the city was dangerous so I didn't go out at night.
3 In Barcelona, we were hungry at 6p.m. so we looked for a restaurant.

a) Big mistake – we went out on the last night and it was great!
b) Big mistake – they only open at 9p.m.!
c) Big mistake – it was cold at night!

B Underline *so* and *because* in sentences 1–3 above. Which word answers the question *why*?

C Underline the correct alternative.

1 We walked *so/because* there were no buses.
2 There were no buses *so/because* we walked.

8A Add *so* or *because* to the sentences.

1 Our plane was at eleven we got to the airport at quarter past ten.
2 I didn't book a hotel I didn't have time.
3 We went to New Zealand in July we have school holidays in the summer.
4 We didn't find any mineral water we drank the local water.

B Work in pairs. What was the 'big mistake' in situations 1–4 above? Write your ideas.

1 Big mistake – the check-in closed at ten so we ...

▶ **FUNCTION** | giving directions   ▶ **VOCABULARY** | prepositions   ▶ **LEARN TO** | use examples

VOCABULARY prepositions

1A Match the prepositions in the box with pictures A–H.

on the right of *B*   on the left of
in front of   near   behind   between
next to   opposite

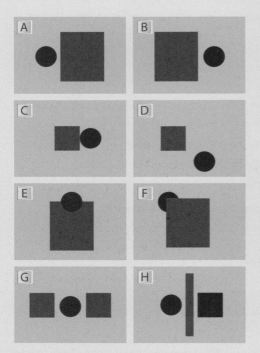

B Work in pairs and take turns. Choose a picture and ask about it.
A: Where's the ball in picture G?
B: It's between the boxes.

2A Tick the sentences that are true for your class.

1 There are windows next to the door.
2 The teacher usually stands behind a table.
3 I sit opposite another student.
4 There's a noticeboard on the right of the door.
5 Our coats and jackets are near the window.
6 My bag is between my table and another table.

B Change the other sentences to make them true for your class.

FUNCTION giving directions

3A ▶ 8.4 Listen to three conversations. What does the person want to find? Write the number of the conversation next to the food.
vegetables ___   bread ___   fish___   fruit *1*   cereal ___   cakes ___
snacks ___   meat _____

B Listen again. Match places a)–f) with the food. Do <u>not</u> use two of the places.
fruit *f*   bread ___   cereal ___   cakes ___

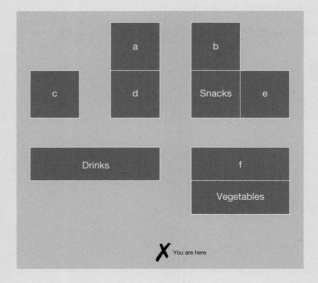

4A Complete the conversation with the words in the box.

~~Excuse~~ behind where see Let over of Do

A: ¹ _Excuse_ me, ² _____ 's the fruit?

B: ³ _____ you ⁴ _____ the vegetables ⁵ _____ there?

A: Yes.

B: The vegetables are in front ⁶ _____ the fruit. Over there.

A: ⁷ _____ me check. The fruit's ⁸ _____ the vegetables.

B: Yes, that's right.

B Work in pairs and practise the conversation.

▉▶ page 132 **LANGUAGEBANK**

LEARN TO use examples

5A ▶ 8.5 Listen and complete the conversations.

1 A: Vegetables? ¹ _____ are they?

   B: Vegetables ... you ² _____, tomatoes, potatoes, carrots.

   A: Oh, vegetables.

2 B: Do you see the snacks?

   A: Snacks? I don't know 'snacks'.

   B: Snacks, for ³ _____, chocolate, nuts and crisps.

   A: Oh, I understand.

3 A: Cereal? What's ⁴ _____?

   B: Cereal. ⁵ _____ Corn Flakes.

❝ speakout TIP

When you don't know a word, examples can help. Use the phrases *you know*, *like* and *for example* to give examples.

B Work in pairs and practise the conversations.

C Work in pairs and take turns. Student A: choose one type of food below and ask Student B about it. Student B: ask for an example.

meat   fruit   vegetables   dairy

A: *Where's the meat?*

B: *Meat? For example?*

A: *You know, chicken, beef, lamb.*

B: *Oh, meat!*

SPEAKING

6A Write the six types of food in <u>your</u> supermarket diagram.

meat   fish   dairy

sweets   bread   fruit

Your supermarket

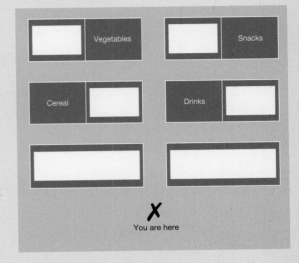

Your partner's supermarket

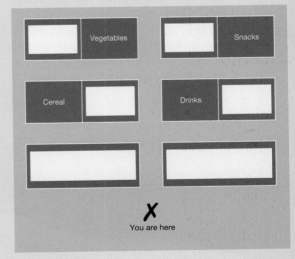

B Work in pairs and take turns. Ask and answer about the food in your partner's supermarket. Write the food in the correct place.

A: *Excuse me, where's the meat?*

B: *It's in front of the ...*

DVD PREVIEW

1A Complete the holiday questionnaire. Tick the sentences that are true for you.

On holiday, I always:

read about the place. ◯   take bus tours. ◯

take a lot of photos. ◯

go out in the evenings. ◯

relax and do nothing. ◯

B Work in pairs and compare your answers.

2 Read the programme information. Are sentences 1–4 true (T) or false (F)?

1 *Little Britain* is funny.
2 A woman plays the tour guide Carol.
3 Carol is friendly.
4 This episode is in Spain.

BBC Little Britain Abroad

The BBC comedy show, *Little Britain*, is about British people in typical situations. Carol Beer (the actor, David Walliams) is often on the show. Carol is always bored and is usually rude to people. In this episode, she is a tour guide for a group of British tourists on holiday in Majorca, Spain.

▶ DVD VIEW

3A Work in pairs and look at the photos. Which woman is Carol?

B Watch the DVD to check your answer.

C Watch the DVD again and number the phrases in the order you hear them.

a) questions or problems __
b) look to your right   __
c) stop the coach   __
d) Sunsearchers Holidays _1_
e) Welcome to Spain   __
f) fun, fun, fun   __
g) get out   __

D Discuss in pairs. What do you think the man and woman do next?

speakout a bad holiday story

4A Work in pairs and look at the pictures. Why did the man have a bad holiday? Use the words/phrases in the box below.

| bored   it rained   noisy   expensive   missed the plane |

B ▶ 8.6 Listen to the man tell the story. Which picture is different from his story?

C Listen again and tick the key phrases you hear.

key phrases
I missed my (plane/train/bus).
I arrived (in Honolulu) one (hour/day/week) late.
I lost my (passport/money/bags).
It rained for (the first three days/all week).
I stayed in (my hotel room/the café) (all day).
The hotel was (noisy/expensive/dirty).
The food was (bad/expensive).
I was very happy to go home.

5A Work in pairs and change three things about the story. Use the key phrases and practise telling your story to each other.

B Work with a new partner. Take turns to tell your stories. How many differences can you find?

writeback a holiday story

6A Read the story and underline six positive things.

Last year we went to Edinburgh on holiday, and I didn't have a good time.

We took a boat from Dublin to Holyhead in Wales, and then a train to Edinburgh. In Holyhead, we were hungry, so we went to a restaurant in the station. The food was great and the waiter was very nice, but we were there for too long and we missed our train. There were no other trains that day, so we stayed in the station.

The next day, we arrived in Edinburgh. We were very tired but the weather was good and the place was beautiful. We were happy - for one hour! Our hotel was lovely and the people were friendly, but then I became ill and I was in bed for five days. We were there for one week. It was a very long week.

B Write your own bad holiday story. Use 70–100 words.

C Read other students' stories. Which one was really bad?

PAST SIMPLE: IRREGULAR VERBS

1A Complete the sentences about the past.

1 I / meet / a friend in a café yesterday.
   I met a friend in a café yesterday.
2 Two students / come / to class late for this lesson.
3 I / think / English was difficult, but it's easy.
4 I / go / home by train last night.
5 I / not sit / here last lesson.
6 I / not have / breakfast at home.
7 I / see / the teacher in a supermarket yesterday.

B Change the sentences so they are true for you.

C Work in pairs. Student A: read your sentences. Student B: listen and say your sentence.
A: *I met a friend in a restaurant yesterday.*
B: *I didn't meet a friend yesterday.*

PREPOSITIONS OF PLACE

2A Work in pairs. Complete the sentences with the words in the box.

class	home	car	work
street	bike	Bangkok	holiday

1 **In the morning I have** two coffees. I have my first coffee at _____ and then my second coffee at _____.
2 **I always listen to music** in my _____, but not on my _____, because it's too dangerous.
3 **I was on** _____ in _____ last year.
4 **I like speaking English** with the teacher in _____, but I don't like speaking with people in the _____.

B Work alone. Write four sentences about you. Start with the words in bold in Exercise 2A and use *in*, *on* or *at*.
In the morning I have tea at home but I drink water at work.

C Work in pairs and compare your sentences.

HOLIDAY ACTIVITIES

3A Add vowels to complete the activities.

1 g_o_ c_a_mp_i_ng
2 sp__ _k __ngl__sh
3 s_ _ _ld b_ _ _ld_ngs
4 dr__nk th__ l__c__l w__t__r
5 __ _t th__ l__c__l f_ _ _d
6 b_ _ __ll
7 h__v_ __ g_ __d t__m__
8 m_ _ _t th__ l__c__l p_ _ __pl__

B Work in pairs. Which activities above do you do:
• on a family holiday in your country with not a lot of money?
• on a weekend city break?
• in a different country?

PAST SIMPLE: QUESTIONS

4A Find and correct the mistakes in the questions about last weekend. One question is correct.

1 Did you had a good weekend?
   Did you have a good weekend?
2 What did you?
3 Met you any friends?
4 Where did you went?
5 a) Did you buy anything?
   b) What you buy?
6 a) You did see a film at the cinema or on TV?
   b) What were it?

B Work in pairs and take turns. Ask and answer the questions.

PREPOSITIONS

5A Put the letters in bold in the correct order to make prepositions.

1 The tree is on the **thirg** of the shop.
2 The tree is **etenweb** the shop and the car.
3 The road is **txne** to the house.
4 The car is on the **flet** of the shop.
5 The man is **hibden** the house.
6 The woman is in **tornf** of the shop.

B Look at sentences 1–6 in Exercise 5A and find three mistakes in the picture.

GIVING DIRECTIONS

6A Complete the conversation with the words in the box.

~~are~~	next	the	no	of	near
there	left				

A: Excuse me, where *are* the vegetables?
B: Do you see the fruit over?
A: Where?
B: Over there, the magazines.
A: Yes, I see it.
B: Well, the vegetables are to the fruit. On the left.
A: Let me check that. They're on the left the fruit.
B: Right.
A: On right?
B: No, you were right. On the.
A: I see. Thank you.
B: problem.

B Work in pairs and practise the conversation.

READING AND GRAMMAR

1A Read the article. What happened to Jim Black?

Businessman, 35, dies in hotel

This morning, Rose Green, a cleaner at the Adolfi Hotel, Edinburgh, found millionaire businessman Jim Black dead behind the hotel. Police think he died between 10 o'clock and midnight last night. Mr Black and his wife, Carla, were at the hotel with Black's business partner, Mike Brown.

B Complete the police's questions to Mike Brown.

1 be / you / Jim / friends?
Were you and Jim friends?
2 you / see / Jim / yesterday afternoon?
3 you / have / dinner / Jim and Carla?
4 What time / you / go / your room?
5 Where / be / you / between ten o'clock and midnight?

C Read Mike's police statement and answer questions 1–5 above.

Witness Statement

Jim Black was a good friend and we were business partners. We sometimes visited places together at weekends – me, Jim and his wife Carla. Carla didn't like me, and she wasn't happy with Jim. I think Carla killed Jim.

Yesterday afternoon I played tennis with Jim for an hour. We started at two o'clock and then at half past three, we went to our rooms in the hotel. I met Jim and Carla at seven o'clock in the restaurant. Jim was very quiet, but Carla talked a lot. I think she was angry with Jim. We ate dinner together and after that I went to my room at ten. I think Jim went out. I didn't go to bed. I wasn't tired and so I listened to the radio. I went to bed at half past eleven.

Mike Brown

Mike Brown

2A Complete Carla's police statement with the past form of the verbs in brackets.

Witness Statement

Jim ¹ *was* (be) my husband. Jim and Mike ² _____ (be) in business together, but they ³ _____ (not be) friends. Mike ⁴ _____ (not like) Jim.

Yesterday afternoon they ⁵ _____ (play) tennis. I ⁶ _____ (walk) to the shops and then I ⁷ _____ (go) back to the hotel at half past four and ⁸ _____ (write) some letters. Jim ⁹ _____ (come) back at six. He ¹⁰ _____ (not talk) to me. He was very angry. We ¹¹ _____ (meet) Mike for dinner at seven. Jim was very quiet, so I talked a lot. We ¹² _____ (have) dinner, then Mike went to his room at ten. Jim and I danced from ten to eleven, and then Jim ¹³ _____ (want) a walk. He went out and I went to our room. I ¹⁴ _____ (be) very tired, so I went to bed. The next morning Jim was dead. I think Mike killed my husband .

Carla Black

Carla Black

B Underline two differences between Carla's and Mike's statements.

C Work in pairs and check your answers.

LISTENING AND GRAMMAR

3A ▶ R4.1 Listen to five people at the Adolfi Hotel and complete the times in the table.

Name	Information	Time
1 Receptionist	a) Mr Black and Mr Brown went out.	1.45
	b) They went back to their hotel rooms.	____
2 Waiter	Two men and a woman left the restaurant.	____
3 Hotel guest	The radio was on in the Blacks' room.	____
4 Night receptionist	a) Mr Black went out.	____
	b) Another man went out.	____
5 Hotel guest	I came back to the hotel.	____

B Listen again. Are the sentences true (T) or false (F)?

1 Mr Black came back to the hotel alone. *F*
2 A man and a woman danced for half an hour in the restaurant.
3 Two people went out of the hotel at 10.15p.m.
4 The other person was Mr Brown.
5 The other person was a woman.

C Work in pairs. Who do you think killed Jim Black?

SPEAKING

4A Work in groups. Students A and B: turn to page 150. Other students: you are the police. Read the information and put the words in 1–4 in the correct order to make questions.

On Monday at half past one in the afternoon there was a robbery at a clothes shop. Police think it was two students from your class. The students say they were at a restaurant.

1 restaurant / arrive / What / at / you / the / did / time?
2 name / was / the / restaurant's / What?
3 you / did / eat / What?
4 cost / much / it / How / did?

B Write two more questions for Students A and B.

C Ask your questions to Student A. Then ask the questions to Student B. Check their answers are the same.

SOUNDS: /ʌ/ AND /ʊ/

5A ▶ R4.2 Listen to the sounds and the words. Then listen and repeat.

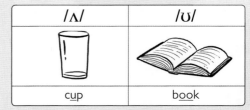

/ʌ/	/ʊ/
cup	book

B ▶ R4.3 Listen and put the words in the box in the correct group. Then listen and repeat.

lunch	put	good	month	country
cook	hungry	look	colour	full

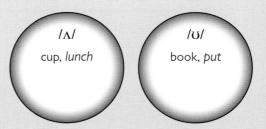

/ʌ/
cup, *lunch*

/ʊ/
book, *put*

6A Work in pairs. Complete the words and circle the sound in each word.

	/ʌ/
four family words	m(o)ther ____
	b____
	h____
	s____
a type of transport in a city	b____
a big country	R____
two days of the week	S____
	M____
a number	o____

	/ʊ/
a sport	f____
you read it and like it	a g____
	b____
two signs on a door	P____
	P____
a month	J____
a food	s____

B Work with another pair and compare.

UNIT 9

SPEAKING
❭ Find the right gift
❭ Talk about how you spend money
❭ Ask people to do things
❭ Describe a favourite possession

LISTENING
❭ Listen to a radio programme about shopping mistakes
❭ Listen to someone shopping
❭ Watch a BBC programme about the iPod

READING
❭ Read a website forum about gift-giving around the world

WRITING
❭ Write photos captions
❭ Write about a favourite possession

BBC content
▯ Video podcast: Do you like shopping?
◉ DVD: Days That Shook The World

UNIT 9

shopping

▶ The right gift   p96

▶ A waste of money   p98

▶ What would you like?   p100

▶ Days That Shook The World p102

► **GRAMMAR** | *like, love, hate + -ing*   ► **VOCABULARY** | activities   ► **HOW TO** | talk about likes and dislikes

What's the right gift in your country?

A visitor to your country wants to give a gift. What's the right gift in your country? We asked you to give us your ideas.

Gifts are very important in Japan. We always wrap gifts but we don't like using white paper because it's unlucky. Never give four gifts. The word 'four' in Japanese is 'shi' and means death. People like pens – they are easy to carry and they mean 'learning'. **Hitomi, Japan**

When people give gifts, we often say 'no' at first. We never open a gift in front of the giver. We wait and open it later. We always use two hands to give a present. **Khun, Thailand**

In Mexico, people like gifts, especially gifts from a different country. People like giving flowers but we don't give red or yellow flowers because red and yellow are unlucky. **Chantico, Mexico**

In the UK, we usually open gifts immediately. British people love getting chocolates or flowers, but red roses are for lovers. Nowadays 'activity' gifts are popular, for example theatre tickets or a dinner for two. **Susan, UK**

READING

1 Work in pairs and discuss. When do you give gifts? Who do you give gifts to?

2A Read the text. Which things are the same as your country?

B Work in pairs and cover the text. Which country/countries are the sentences about?

1 Always use two hands. *Thailand*
2 Chocolates are good.
3 Don't give four gifts.
4 It isn't OK to open gifts in front of the person.
5 People like flowers.
6 Yellow roses are a bad idea.
7 Pens are good gifts.
8 People often give 'activities'.

C Read the text again and check your ideas.

D Complete the sentences. Then work in pairs and tell your partner.

1 In my country, good gifts are ...
2 On my last birthday, I got ...
3 On my friend's last birthday, I gave him/her ...

⟫ page 146 **PHOTOBANK**

GRAMMAR *like, love, hate + -ing*

3A Look at the sentences. Put the verbs in bold on the line.

We **don't like** using white paper.
People **like** giving flowers.
British people **love** getting chocolates or flowers.
I **hate** buying gifts for people. I always buy boring gifts.

¹ *love*	2	3	4
✓✓	✓	✗	✗✗

B Look at the table and underline the correct alternative in rules 1 and 2.

I/You/We	love like	pens.
He/She	doesn't like hates	buying gifts.

Rules:
1 Use *love, (not) like, hate + singular/plural* noun.
2 Use *love, (not) like, hate + verb/verb + -ing*

C ▶ 9.1 Listen to the sentences. Then listen and repeat.

⟫ page 134 **LANGUAGEBANK**

PRACTICE

4A Complete the sentences with the *-ing* form of the verbs in the box. Pay attention to the spelling.

~~eat~~   live   get up   go   read   watch   wrap   have

1 I love ___*eating*___ vegetables.
2 I hate _____ sport on TV.
3 I like _____ two sisters.
4 I don't like _____ in bed.
5 I like _____ to parties.
6 I love _____ in a city.
7 I don't like _____ before eight o'clock.
8 I hate _____ gifts.

B Tick the sentences that are true for you. Change the ones that are false.

I hate eating vegetables.

C Work in pairs and find two things the same for you and your partner.

VOCABULARY activities

5A Write the *-ing* form of the verbs to make activities.

1 run<u>ning</u>
2 relax_____
3 play_____ computer games
4 cook_____
5 take_____ photos
6 go_____ to the theatre
7 swim_____
8 chat_____ online
9 camp_____
10 go_____ on long walks

B Which activities above do you usually do:

• outside?   • in special clothes?
• inside?   • with a machine?
• with someone?

C Work in pairs and take turns. Ask and answer about the activities. Start with *Do you like ... ?*

A: *Do you like running?*
B: *No, I hate it. I never run.*

speakout TIP

Short answers give a lot of information. Look at the different ways to answer the question, *Do you like ... ? No, not at all. No, not really. It depends. Yes, I do. Yes, sometimes. Yes, a lot.* Write them in your phrasebook.

SPEAKING

6A Look at the website. Which of the activities are in the photos?

B Work in pairs and take turns. Ask questions to complete the information.

	love	like	not like	hate
animals		✔		
dancing				
relaxing				
sweets				
cooking				
being outside				
eating out				
watching plays				
driving fast				
doing exercise				

A: *Do you like animals?*
B: *Yes, I do.*

C Work alone and choose the best activity gift from the website for your partner. Then tell your partner the gift.

D Tell the class about your activity gift. Was it right for you? Why/Why not?

Activity-gifts4u.com Shop now ▶

Give your friends and family a very special gift. Here are our top ten:

▶ hot-air balloon trip

▶ theatre evening

▶ driving a Formula-1 car

▶ salsa lessons

▶ sushi-making class

▶ chocolate-making class

▶ bird-watching tour

▶ dinner for two

▶ one-to-one tennis class

▶ day at a beauty spa

VOCABULARY money

1A Work in pairs and discuss. Do you like shopping? Why/Why not?

B Work in pairs. Look at the verbs in bold and underline the correct alternative.

1 You see something in a shop. You want it, but you don't need it. Do you:
  a) walk out of the shop?
  b) *buy/sell* it and then never use it?

2 You have a lot of things at home. You don't need everything. Do you:
  a) *buy/sell* things on the internet?
  b) give things to friends?

3 How much did you *pay/cost* for your last coffee or tea? Do you think it was:
  a) too much?
  b) the right price?

4 How much does transport *pay/cost* you every week? Is this:
  a) too much?
  b) OK?

5 It's your birthday. You *get/give* an expensive gift, but you hate it. Do you:
  a) keep it but never use it?
  b) give it to someone else?

C Work in pairs and take turns. Ask and answer questions 1–5.

2A Write the past forms of the verbs. Check in your dictionary.

1 buy *bought*
2 sell _____
3 pay _____
4 cost _____
5 give _____
6 get _____

B ▶ 9.2 Listen and repeat the verbs.

C Work in pairs and take turns. Student A: say a verb. Student B: say the past form.

▶ page 147 **PHOTOBANK**

LISTENING

3A Match the words in the box with pictures A–E.

> hat   lamp   tent   drums   exercise bike

B Look at the pictures. Do you like the objects or do you think they are a waste of money?

C ▶ 9.3 Listen to people talk about their shopping mistakes. Match speakers 1–5 with pictures A–E.

1 ___   2 ___   3 ___   4 ___   5 ___

D Work in groups. Look at the shopping mistakes. Choose one mistake and tell the other students about it.

wrong size   didn't use it   didn't like it

it didn't work   too small   too big

broke it   wrong colour

A: I bought a bike. It was a very good bike, but I didn't use it so I gave it to a friend.

GRAMMAR object pronouns

4A Complete the sentences with the words in the box. Do <u>not</u> use one of the words.

~~me~~ you them us it her him

1 My wife bought <u>me</u> an exercise bike for my birthday. I used _____ three times.
2 My boyfriend wanted to go camping so I bought _____ a tent.
3 I phoned _____ yesterday, but she didn't answer.
4 He loves those drums. He plays _____ every day.
5 My mother gave _____ a lamp, but we didn't like it .

B Look at the sentence and complete the table.

<u>She</u> phoned <u>me</u> last night.

subject   object
pronoun   pronoun

subject pronoun	object pronoun
I	_me_
you	_____
he	_____
she	_____
it	_____
we	_____
they	_____

C Underline the correct alternatives in the rule.

> **Rule:**
> Use a subject pronoun *before/after* a verb. Use an object pronoun *before/after* a verb.

D ▶ 9.4 Listen to the sentences. Notice how we link the verbs and the object pronouns. Then listen and repeat.

I used it.   I bought him a tent.
She gave us a lamp.   I phoned her yesterday.

▮▶ page 134 **LANGUAGEBANK**

PRACTICE

5A Complete the sentences with an object pronoun.
1 My bag? I bought ___it___ in Spain.
2 My shoes? I got _____ from a shop near here.
3 My mobile? I don't often use _____ .
4 My last birthday? My sister gave _____ a pen.
5 Did you see me last night? I saw _____ .
6 Homework in our class? Our teacher gives _____ homework every night.
7 A student called Maria? I don't know _____ .
8 A student called Stefan? I know _____ .

B Change the sentences so they are true for you.
My bag? I bought it in Portugal.

C Work in pairs and compare your answers.

WRITING captions

6A Which of captions 1–4 goes with the photo?

1 New women's Silver Sports trainers, size 38
 I got the new trainers in Rome. The new trainers are the wrong size.

2 A signed photo of Johnny Depp
 I met Johnny Depp in Los Angeles last year. Johnny Depp gave me two photos and I want to sell one of the photos.

3 For sale: my Honda 500T
 I bought my Honda 500T in 1998. My Honda 500T is a beautiful motorbike but I don't use my Honda 500T much now.

4 The 2009 Tour Book of Beyoncé I AM
 I saw Beyoncé in Caracas. Beyoncé was fantastic but my new flat is too small for all my books.

B Rewrite the captions using pronouns.

1 New women's Silver Sports trainers, size **38**.
     them   *They*
 I got ~~the new trainers~~ in Rome. ~~The new trainers~~ are the wrong size.

C Work in pairs. Write captions for two objects to sell online.

D Work in groups and read your captions. Which object do you think is best?

SPEAKING

7A Work alone and think of examples of the things below:
• something that was a waste of money.
• something big you bought last month.
• something you really want to buy now.
• a shop you think is great.
• something you sold because you didn't like it.
• something you gave to someone for free.
• something very expensive you bought.

B Work in pairs and compare your answers.
A: Tell me something that was a waste of money.
B: An electric guitar. I bought it but I never played it.

WHAT WOULD YOU LIKE?

► **FUNCTION** | making requests   ► **VOCABULARY** | shopping departments   ► **LEARN TO** | use hesitation phrases

VOCABULARY   shopping departments

1A Work in pairs and look at pictures A–F. Where do you buy these things in your town/city?

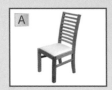  
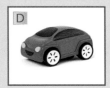  

B Look at the store guide and match the departments with pictures A–F.

STORE GUIDE

THIRD FLOOR (3) ▼
Furniture & Lighting
Bed & Bath
Travel & Luggage
Sky Restaurant

SECOND FLOOR (2) ▼
Children's Clothes & Shoes
Toys
Computers & Phones
Home Entertainment
Sports

FIRST FLOOR (1) ▼
Women's Clothes & Shoes
Star Café

GROUND FLOOR (G) ▼
Beauty
Jewellery & Watches
Menswear & Shoes

C ▶ 9.5 Listen and repeat the departments.

2 Work in pairs and take turns. Student A: you are a customer. Ask about one of the objects below. Which department is it? Student B: you are a shop assistant. Answer Student A.

a laptop   a dress   a DVD

a child's T-shirt   a football   a necklace

A: I want to buy a laptop. Which department is it?
B: Computers and phones.

FUNCTION   making requests

3A ▶ 9.6 Listen to the conversations and tick the correct answers.

1 Tom wants a World Cup:
  a) T-shirt.   b) computer game.
  c) DVD.

2 Lisa goes first to:
  a) the Sports Department.   b) Home Entertainment.
  c) Computers and Phones.

3 Lisa:
  a) finds a gift for Tom.   b) doesn't find a gift.
  c) finds three gifts.

B ▶ 9.7 Complete the sentences. Then listen and check.

1 _____ would you like for your birthday?
2 _____ you like a football shirt?
3 I'd _____ a DVD.

C Look at the table and underline the correct alternatives in the rules.

I'd	like	a computer game.
Would you		this DVD?

Rules:
1 *I'd like* means *I like/ I want*.
2 *I'd like* is *polite/ not polite*.

▮▮▶ page 134 **LANGUAGEBANK**

5A Look at the sentences from the conversation. Underline six different ways to give yourself time to think.

A: What would you like for your birthday?

B: <u>Oh, I don't know.</u> Let me think …

B: Um ... well … maybe something from the World Cup.

A: Which DVD is best?

E: Er ... let me see ... this one has all the important games.

speakout TIP

When you need time to think, use hesitation phrases: *Er/ Um … , Let me think/see/look … , Well … .* What sounds or words do you use in your language to do this?

B ▶ 9.9 Listen to the questions and use hesitation phrases before you answer.

C Work in pairs. Student A: turn to page 150. Student B: turn to page 152. Ask and answer the questions. Use hesitation phrases.

SPEAKING

6A Work in pairs and complete the conversation.

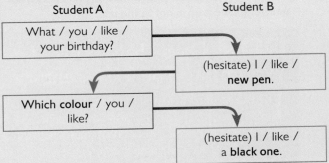

Student A | Student B

What / you / like / your birthday?

(hesitate) I / like / **new pen.**

Which colour / you / like?

(hesitate) I / like / a **black one.**

B Work in pairs and take turns. Practise the conversation.

C Work alone. Write three things you would like for your birthday.

D Work in pairs and practise the conversation with different gifts. Change the words in bold.

4A Put the words in the correct order to make conversations.

1 A: like / you / Would / coffee / a?

B: I'd / tea / but / No / a / thanks, / like

2 A: like / her / Sue / birthday / What / would / for?

B: think / she'd / bike / I / like / a

3 A: a / you / Would / break / like?

B: let's / Yes, / for / an / half / stop / hour

4 A: sweaters / these / Can / of / I / have / one?

B: like / you / colour / Yes, / which / would?

B ▶ 9.8 Listen to the intonation and circle the correct letter: P (polite) or NP (not polite). Then listen again and repeat.

1 Would you like a coffee?   P   NP

2 Would you like a coffee?   P   NP

3 I'd like a tea, please.   P   NP

4 I'd like a tea, please.   P   NP

C Work in pairs and take turns. Student A: read out a request from Exercise 4B. Student B: listen and say *polite* or *not polite.*

DVD PREVIEW

1A Put items A–F in order on the timeline.

1950   1960   1970   1980   1990   2000

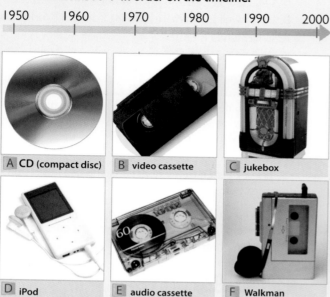

A **CD (compact disc)**   B **video cassette**   C **jukebox**

D **iPod**   E **audio cassette**   F **Walkman**

B Read the programme information and check your answers. One item is <u>not</u> in the text.

BBC Days That Shook The World: Into The 21st Century

In the nineteen-fifties people listened to music on jukeboxes; in the sixties and seventies it was the audio cassette. When the Sony Walkman and the compact disc, or CD, arrived in the nineteen-eighties, there was a big change in the music world, but that was only the start. Apple introduced its first MP3 player, the iPod, in October 2001, and the music world changed forever. This episode of the BBC's *Days That Shook The World* looks at how this small machine changed our lives.

▶ DVD VIEW

2A Watch the DVD. Which items in the photos are in the programme?

B Work in pairs and choose the correct alternative. Then watch the DVD again to check your answers.

1 People walked around with thousands of their *best/favourite* songs …

2 … the iPod was really *different/good*. It was fun.

3 It looked good with its touch control and *small/white* headphones.

4 Students listened to their *lessons/teachers* at home.

5 *People/Tourists* listened to audio tours in cities.

6 Bands used the internet to *send/give* their music to people's computers and MP3 players.

7 The *old/new* technology of the eighties and nineties is now rubbish.

C Work in pairs and discuss. What do you listen to on your music player?

speak**out** a possession

3A Think about one of your favourite possessions. Use the questions below to make notes about it.

Possession: _____

- Where did you get it?
- Where is it now?
- What do you do with it?
- Why do you like it?

Other information: _____

B Work in pairs and take turns. Ask and answer the questions above.

C ▶ 9.10 Listen to someone talk about a favourite possession and answer the questions in Exercise 3A.

D Listen again and tick the key phrases you hear.

key**phrases**

One of my favourite (things/possessions) is …
It's (very small /big/red).
I keep it (in my bag/pocket/at home).
I bought it (last year/in New York).
(My brother/wife/best friend) gave it to me …
for (my birthday/Christmas)
I like it because it's (easy to use/useful/beautiful).

4A Work with a new partner. Practise talking about a favourite possession. Use the key phrases to help.

B Work in groups and take turns. Tell other students about your favourite possession.

write**back** a favourite possession

5A Read the text. Which questions from Exercise 3A does it answer?

My bike

One of my favourite things is my bike. My friends gave it to me for my eighteenth birthday. It's a 1990s *TREK* 720. It's now twenty years old but I like it because it's good in all types of weather. It's also good in the city. I ride it to work every day and I keep it in the street near my workplace. At home I keep it in the garden. It's not new, but it's a fantastic little bike.

B Write a description of a favourite possession. Write 50–80 words.

LIKE, LOVE, HATE + -ING

1A Complete the questions.

1 you / like / read?
   Do you like reading?
2 What / you / like / read?
3 What / TV programme / you / like / watch?
4 Who / you / like / phone?
5 What / you / like / eat / for dinner?
6 you / like / travel / by plane?
7 What / sport / like / do?
8 What / music / like / listen / to?

B Work in pairs and take turns. Ask and answer the questions.

ACTIVITIES

2A Add the vowels to complete the activities.

1 c__mp__ng
2 c__ __k__ng
3 g__ __ng __ __n l__ng w__lks
4 ch__tt__ng __nl__n__
5 r__nn__ng
6 g__ __ng t__ th__ th__ __tr__
7 pl__y__ng c__mp__t__r g__m__s
8 r__l__x__ng
9 t__k__ng ph__t__s
10 sw__mm__ng

B Work in pairs and take turns. Student A: choose an activity. Think of the place you do it and an object you need. Student B: ask questions and guess the activity.

B: Where do you do it?
A: In the countryside.
B: What do you need?
A: A tent.
B: Camping?
A: Yes!

MONEY

3A Put the letters in the correct order to make verbs.

1 ybu *buy*   4 tocs
2 vegi   5 etg
3 lels   6 apy

B Complete the sentences with the correct form of the verbs above.

1 I *buy* a new mobile phone once a year.
2 Food ____ too much.
3 My manager ____ me well.
4 I ____ money to poor people.
5 For my birthday I always ____ clothes from my family.
6 I never ____ things to my friends.

C Tick the sentences in Exercise 3B that you agree with. Then compare with a partner.

OBJECT PRONOUNS

4A Match sentences 1–6 with a)–f). Use the underlined pronoun to help.

1 I don't know <u>them</u>. *f*
2 I hate <u>it</u>.
3 <u>They</u> bring us food.
4 I like <u>him</u>.
5 <u>They</u> often phone me.
6 I saw <u>her</u> yesterday.

a) my sister
b) my friends
c) waiters
d) ice cream
e) Robert Pattinson
f) The Rolling Stones

B Write people and things that are true for you for 1–6.

1 I don't know them.
   The students in the next class.

C Work in pairs and take turns. Student A: say one thing on your list. Student B: say the sentence that matches.

A: Elvis Presley.
B: You like him.
A: Yes!

SHOPPING DEPARTMENTS

5A Correct one spelling mistake in each department name.

1   Jewellery & Waches
2   Computers & Fones
3   Furniture & Liting
4   Travel & Lugage
5   Home Entertenment
6   Bed & Batth
7   Menswhere & Shoes
8   Beautey
9   Childrins clothes & Shoes
10 Toyz

B Work in pairs and discuss. What's your favourite department in a store? What do you usually buy there?

MAKING REQUESTS

6A Find and correct six mistakes in the conversation.

A: ~~I can~~ help you? *Can I*
B: Yes, I would this **pen**.
A: OK. Is he a present?
B: Er … yes.
A: Which wrapping paper you would like – **red or green**?
B: I'd like the **green** paper.
A: Where is the gift for?
B: For I. Today is my birthday!

B Work in pairs and practise the conversation.

C Work alone. Change the words in bold for your part (A or B).

D Work in pairs. Practise the new conversation.

BBC VIDEO PODCAST

Watch people talking about going shopping on ActiveBook or on the website.

Authentic BBC interviews

www.pearsonELT.com/speakout

UNIT 10

SPEAKING
- Discuss the best job for you
- Talk about plans
- Start and end conversations
- Talk about when you tried something new

LISTENING
- Listen to job interviews
- Listen to street interviews about people's goals
- Listen to people start and end conversations
- Watch a BBC comedy about a funny woman

READING
- Read about interesting jobs

WRITING
- Check your writing
- Write an interview about something new

BBC CONTENT
- Video podcast: What did you want to be?
- DVD: Miranda

UNIT
10

plans

▶ A new job   p106

▶ Time for a change   p108

▶ Hello and goodbye   p110

▶ Miranda   p112

▶ **GRAMMAR** | can/can't   ▶ **VOCABULARY** | collocations   ▶ **HOW TO** | talk about ability

VOCABULARY collocations

1A Work in pairs and complete the word webs with the verbs in the box. Which activities are in the photos?

> ~~cook~~ ride speak drive play make read remember

dinner
(1 _cook_)
Italian food   rice

tennis
(2 _____)
golf   football

English
(3 _____)
Spanish   two languages

words in Arabic
(4 _____)
a map   music

English words
(5 _____)
information   phone numbers

a pizza
(6 _____)
clothes   a coffee

a bus
(7 _____)
a taxi   a car

a motorbike
(8 _____)
a bike   a horse

B Work in pairs and take turns. Student A: say a verb. Student B: say three nouns that go with the verb. Student A: try to add more nouns.

A: read
B: read music, read a map, read Arabic
A: read a book, read a newspaper

READING

2A Read the job adverts below. Which job is best for you? Which one is not good for you? Why?

JOBS

1 Tour guide

Tourist service needs a tour guide to take small groups of tourists on visits to the old town. You need to speak English and one other language, and you need a good memory for facts. Driving licence also needed. Contact us at tourguides extra@hayoo.com.

2 Pizza delivery person

Can you ride a motorbike? Do you know the city well? Are you friendly but can you also work alone? We are a small pizza business. We need a delivery person to take pizzas to people's houses. Sometimes we need help in the kitchen, cleaning and cooking. Contact us at superza@zmail.com.

3 Singer/Guitarist

We're a student rock band and last week we lost our lead singer/guitarist. There are two of us (on drums and bass guitar) and we play rock music from the 90s and write new songs. Are you a good singer? Can you play guitar? It's also good if you can dance. Email davylee111@bigmail.com or phone 0382 444 1836 and ask for Davy.

B Read about jobs 1–3 again. Correct the sentences below. One sentence is correct.

1a) You need to speak three languages.
 b) You need a car.
2a) You work in the kitchen every day.
 b) You need to live in the city.
3a) The rock band would like a dancer.
 b) The group's songs are from the 90s.

3A ▶ 10.1 Listen to three interviews. Which job do the people want? Do they get the jobs?

B Listen again. Why do/don't they get the jobs?

GRAMMAR *can/can't*

4A Complete the sentences with *can* or *can't*.

	you	sing? make pizzas?
Yes, No,	I	____. ____.

+	I/You/He/She We/They	____	play guitar. drive.
–		____	

B Underline the correct alternative to complete the rule.

Rule:

Use *can* or *can't* to talk about *your ability/activities you do every day.*

C ▶ 10.2 Listen. Then listen and repeat.
1 can   /kən/   *1*
2 can   /kæn/
3 can't   /kɑːnt/

D ▶ 10.3 Listen to six sentences. Which of the sounds (1, 2 or 3) above do you hear? Write the number.

➥ page 136 **LANGUAGEBANK**

PRACTICE

5A Complete the questions with *can.*
1 you / play tennis? *Can you play tennis?*
2 he / sing?
3 Barbara / ride a horse?
4 you / dance?
5 you and your friend / speak Italian?
6 George / read Chinese?

B Write answers to the questions above.
1 No, *I can't* , but *I can* play football.
2 Yes, ____ _____.
3 No, ____ _____.
4 Yes, ____ _____, and ____ _____ sing, too.
5 No, ____ _____, but ____ _____ _____ Spanish.
6 Yes, ____ _____, but ____ _____ speak Chinese.

➥ page 147 **PHOTOBANK**

SPEAKING

6A Work in pairs and look at the quiz. Take turns to ask questions and complete the quiz for your partner.
A: Can you dance?
B: Yes, I can, but not very well.

What is your perfect job?

5 = very well   3 = quite well   1 = not very well   0 = I can't

Can you …

A	B	C
dance …	play football …	play chess …
sing …	play tennis …	read a map …
act …	ride a horse …	speak another
play guitar	run five	language …
or piano …	kilometres …	remember information …

B Turn to the key on page 152. What's the best job for your partner?

C Work in pairs and answer the questions.
1 Do you think the quiz is right about you?
2 What job would you like to do?

A: The quiz says a good job for me is in sports, but I'd like to be a doctor. I like helping people. What about you?
B: I'd like to be a …

VOCABULARY   life changes

1A Read the list of top ten goals. Which ones can you see in the pictures?

Top ten goals

People often want to make changes in their life: their job, their lifestyle, their relationships. They talk about it, they buy a self-help book ... but usually nothing changes, and then a year later the same goal comes back again. They say, 'This time, I'm <u>really</u> going to make a change!'

  We asked our readers: 'What are your goals?' Here are their top ten:

1 stop smoking
2 get fit
3 spend more time with friends and family
4 work less and relax more
5 help others
6 get organised
7 lose weight
8 learn something new
9 save money
10 change jobs

B Read the list again. Work in pairs. Do you want to do any of these things?

A: I want to get organised.
B: Me, too! And I want to ...

LISTENING

2A ▶ 10.4 Listen to five people talk about their goals. Write the number(s) from the list in Exercise 1A next to the name.

1	Tom	_8_	4 Rudi	____
2	Fiona	____	5 Alex	____
3	Liam	____		

B Listen again. Are the sentences true (T) or false (F)?

1 Tom's girlfriend can't cook.
2 He wants to learn Japanese cooking.
3 Fiona wants to work in an office.
4 Liam plans to stop watching TV.
5 Rudi's a good tennis player.
6 He plans to walk a lot.
7 Alex plans to spend more time with her friends.
8 She likes shopping.

C Work in pairs and discuss. Which people are similar to you? Why?

GRAMMAR *be going to*

3A Look at sentences a)–d) and answer the questions.

1 Are they about the present or future?

2 Which are positive (+) and negative (–)?

a) I'm going to learn to cook.

b) My friend Sheila is going to help me.

c) Then you aren't going to save money!

d) Yes, but I'm not going to stop shopping.

B Complete the table.

I'm You'__ She'__	going __	change jobs. work less. get fit.

C Complete the negative form. Put *n't* in the correct place in the sentences.

He is going to be there.

We are going to come.

D ▶ 10.5 Listen and check your answers to Exercises 3B and 3C. Then listen again and repeat. Pay attention to the pronunciation of *going to* /ɡəʊɪŋ tə/.

➡ page 136 **LANGUAGEBANK**

PRACTICE

4A Complete the sentences with *be going to*.

1 After class, / I / have / a coffee.
   After class, I'm going to have a coffee.

2 I / not / do / the homework / tonight.

3 Tonight, / the teacher / watch / TV.

4 I / not / write / any emails / tomorrow.

5 Tomorrow afternoon, / I / relax.

6 On Friday, / my friends and I / see a film.

B Tick the sentences that are true for you. Change the ones that are not true.

C Work in pairs and compare your answers.

A: *After class, I'm going to have a coffee. What about you?*

B: *I'm not going to have a coffee. I'm going to have lunch.*

D Work in groups. Say one thing about your partner's plans and one thing about your plans.

A: *Tomorrow afternoon, Jan's going to relax, but I'm going to play football in the park.*

SPEAKING

5A Look at the picture. Write your five plans or goals in the boxes.

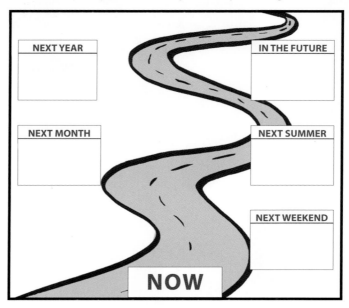

B Work in groups and take turns. Tell other students your plans.

Next summer, I'm going to work in a hotel.

WRITING checking your work

6A Read the email. Find and correct:

• five mistakes with the punctuation/capitalisation.

• five mistakes with the verbs.

> Hi
> hi Elif,
> Thanks for your email. Heres the information about my plans. I'm going be in Istanbul on sunday for three days. Can we to meet? My hotel is the FiveStar in Topsu Street. I going to visit the Blue Mosque on Monday and Id like to look around the markets. Can we have lunch together one day. Are Tuesday good for you? Email me or texted me.
> Jayne

speakout TIP

After you write something, check your writing. You can check punctuation and verbs. What other things can you check?

B Write an email to another student. Give your plans and arrange a time to meet for lunch. Use the email above to help.

C Work in pairs. Check each other's emails. Use your ideas from the Speakout Tip to help.

D Answer your partner's email.

10.3 HELLO AND GOODBYE

▶ **FUNCTION** | conversations ▶ **VOCABULARY** | saying goodbye ▶ **LEARN TO** | respond naturally

2A Complete the conversations with the words in the box. Then check audio script 10.6 on page 160.

~~great~~ going have (x 2) talk around this think friend time

1 A: Hey, this is a ¹_great_ place.
   B: Yes, it's really good. I often come here.

2 B: … Let's have coffee.
   A: OK … wait, is that the ²_____? I'm sorry, I ³_____ a lesson at two.

3 A: Excuse me, do you ⁴_____ the time ?
   B: Yes, it's half past four.
   A: So where are you ⁵_____?

4 B: … I moved to Madrid when I was ten.
   A: I see … oh, look, ⁶_____ is my station.

5 A: What do you ⁷_____ of the music?
   B: It's not bad.

6 A: So are you from ⁸_____ here?

7 B: I'm sorry, I can see an old ⁹_____ over there. Nice to ¹⁰_____ to you.
   A: Oh … and you.

FUNCTION conversations

1A Work in pairs and answer the questions.

1 How do you say hello and goodbye in your country?
2 How do you start a conversation with a stranger? What do you talk about?

B ▶10.6 Listen to the conversations and write friends (F) or strangers (S).

1 ____   2 ____   3 ____

C Listen again. Why does the person end the conversation? Tick the correct reason a)–c).

Conversation 1
a) He wants a coffee.
b) He has a lesson.
c) He has no money for lunch.

Conversation 2
a) She's going to get off the train.
b) She lost her bank card.
c) She doesn't like the man.

Conversation 3
a) She wants to leave the party.
b) She doesn't speak any languages.
c) She thinks he's boring.

B Work in pairs and look at the conversations above. Find:

1 five phrases for starting a conversation
   This is a great place.
2 five phrases for finishing a conversation
   Is that the time?

C ▶10.7 Listen and underline the stressed words. Then listen and repeat.

1 What do you think of the music?
2 Are you from around here?
3 Is that the time?
4 Nice to talk to you.

▶ page 136 **LANGUAGEBANK**

3A Complete the conversations.

Student A | Student B

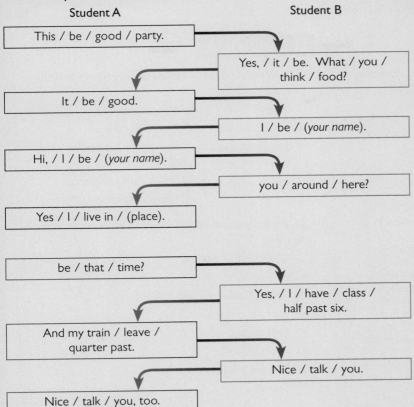

- This / be / good / party.
- Yes, / it / be. What / you / think / food?
- It / be / good.
- I / be / (your name).
- Hi, / I / be / (your name).
- you / around / here?
- Yes / I / live in / (place).
- be / that / time?
- Yes, / I / have / class / half past six.
- And my train / leave / quarter past.
- Nice / talk / you.
- Nice / talk / you, too.

B Work in pairs and take turns to practise the conversations.

LEARN TO respond naturally

4A Work in pairs. How can B respond naturally to A?

1 A: This is a great place.
   B: _____.
2 A: Very nice to meet you.
   B: _____.
3 A: I hope we meet again.
   B: _____.
4 A: Here's my card.
   B: _____.

B ▶ 10.8 Listen and complete the conversations above.

speakout TIP

There are a lot of two-line conversations in English. For example:
A: How are you?
B: Fine, thanks. And you?
Learn these two-line conversations to help your speaking.

C Work in pairs and take turns. Use the prompts below to practise the two-line conversations in Exercise 4A.

my card   great place   meet again   nice to meet

VOCABULARY saying goodbye

5A Complete the phrases for saying goodbye and leaving. Use audio script 10.6 on page 160 to help.

1 see you s__ __ __ __
2 see you i__ two w__ __ __ __ __
3 keep in t__ __ __ __ __
4 b__ __
5 see you l__ __ __ __ __

B Work in pairs and take turns. Student A: say goodbye. Student B: answer with a different phrase.

A: Bye.
B: See you later.

SPEAKING

6A You are going to role-play a party. Work in pairs and write three ways to start a conversation. You can say/ask something about:
- the food   • the music   • the party
- the other person's plans for the weekend
- last weekend

B Role-play the party. Have conversations with other people. After about one minute, finish the conversation politely and move to another person.

Hi, Luca. This is a great …

Hi, Jan. What do you think of the … ?

Hi, Marta. What are your plans for … ?

Nice to chat to you.

Is that the time?

111

DVD PREVIEW

1A Work in pairs and discuss the questions. Use the ideas below to help. What problems can you have when you:

- learn something new?
- change jobs?
- go to a new place?
- spend time with friends?
- try to get fit?

You have the wrong clothes.	You break something.	The teacher doesn't like you.
You make mistakes.	You feel stupid.	It's too expensive.
	You aren't good at it.	You don't understand what to do.
You don't know the people.	You're bored.	

B Read the programme information and answer the questions.

1 What does Miranda want to do?
2 Which things from Exercise 1A does she try?

▶ DVD VIEW

2A Watch the DVD. Match the problems and the places.

1 the gym
2 the restaurant
3 the dance class

a) The teacher didn't like her.
b) She broke things.
c) She didn't understand what to do.
d) She wasn't good at it.
e) She was stuck.

B Which phrases did Miranda say? Write M next to them.

a) Excuse me.   *M*
b) Are you OK?
c) Help! Make it stop please!
d) Sorry about this.
e) Hello again.
f) She is amazing.
g) You are a natural.
h) Really?

C Watch the DVD again to check your answers.

BBC Miranda

Miranda is a BBC comedy show, and Miranda is the star of the show. She's thirty-something, isn't very fit, doesn't like her job, and doesn't have a boyfriend. In this episode Miranda wants to change her life and become the 'New Me.' So she goes to the gym, to dance lessons, and to a Japanese restaurant with her friends ... but for Miranda, there's always a problem!

speakout something new

3A Think about a time when you tried to learn something new. Look at the questions below and make notes:

1 What did you try to learn? When? Why?
2 Did you do it alone or with a friend?
3 Did you have a teacher? Was he or she good?
4 What happened?

B Work in pairs and take turns. Ask and answer the questions above.

C ▶10.9 Listen to a woman talk about learning something new. Answer the questions in Exercise 3A.

D Listen again and tick the key phrases you hear.

keyphrases

I wanted to learn (to play guitar/to cook) because …
I went to a class.
I tried to learn it (alone/with a friend).
I was/wasn't (very) good at it.
The teacher was (great/good/not very good).
After (four/six) months I (played guitar/did it) really well.
I still (do it/play) every day.

4A Work with a new partner and tell each other your stories. Use the key phrases to help.

B Work in groups and take turns. Student A: tell your story. Other students: ask one question.

writeback an interview

5A Read the start of the magazine interview and answer the questions.

1 What did the person try to learn? Why?
2 Do you know how to do this activity?
3 If yes, do you like it? If no, would you like to learn to do it?

Something new

Q: What did you try to learn?
A: How to use *Twitter*.

Q: Why did you want to learn it?
A: Because all my friends use *Twitter*.

Q: When was this?
A: Last summer. I can't remember when exactly.

Q: So, how did you learn?
A: Well, I asked a friend for help.

Q: What happened?
A: We tried …

B Write a magazine interview about another student's learning story.

COLLOCATIONS

1A The verbs are in the wrong sentences. Put them in the correct sentence.

1 I often ~~speak~~ Italian food. *cook*

2 I read tennis every weekend.

3 It's easy to ride maps.

4 I play two languages.

5 I cook all my clothes.

6 I remember my bike to work.

7 I would like to make a bus.

8 It's easy to drive phone numbers.

B Add two more words/phrases to each verb.
cook lunch, cook pasta

C Work in pairs. Which sentences in Exercise 1A are true for you?

CAN/CAN'T

2A Use the words to make five questions with *What ... can ... ?*
What languages can you speak?

languages
songs
sports
food
important dates

cook
speak
play
remember
sing

B Work in pairs and take turns. Ask and answer the questions.

LIFE CHANGES

3A Underline the correct alternative.

1 get *organised*/ new

2 change *smoking/jobs*

3 save *money/weight*

4 learn something *new/others*

5 spend more *jobs/time with friends*

6 work *money/less and relax more*

7 help *organised/others*

8 stop *smoking/fit*

9 lose *weight/time with friends*

10 get *less and relax more/fit*

B Work in pairs and discuss. Which life changes are easy, and which are difficult?
A: I think it's easy to get organised.
B: For me, it's difficult.

BE GOING TO

4A Look at the list. Write the man's plans for the day.
He's going to go to the supermarket. He's going to buy some milk and cheese.

To do:

supermarket — milk, cheese

café — Sue and Jenny

gym

cash machine — 200 euros

newsagent's — newspaper

pharmacy — aspirin

B Write a list of four places you're going to next week.

C Work in pairs. Look at your partner's list and guess what he/she is going to do.
A: The park. OK, you're going to walk in the park.
B: No.
A: You're going to play football.
B: Yes.

SAYING GOODBYE

5 Find and correct the mistakes.

1 See you late.

2 By.

3 See you one week.

4 Keep on touch.

5 See soon

CONVERSATIONS

6A Complete the conversations with the words in the box.

~~are~~ minutes there nice (x 2)
that you do

A: Hi!
B: Oh, hi. How ~~are~~ you?
A: **Good**, thanks. This is a **café**.
B: Yes, I sometimes come here for **lunch**.
A: Really? What you think of the **food**?
B: Er … it's good. Wait, is the time?
A: No, that clock's wrong. It's **two o'clock**.
B: Oh no, my **train** leaves in five!
A: No problem. There's a train every half hour.
B: Sorry, I can see **an old friend** over.
A: Oh, OK. to talk to you.
B: And to you. See soon …

B Work in pairs and practise the conversation.

C Change the words in bold.

D Work with a new partner. Practise the new conversation.
A: Hi!
B: Oh, hi. How are you?
B: Fine, thanks. This is a nice hotel.
A: Yes, I sometimes come here for dinner.

BBC VIDEO PODCAST
Watch people talking about the jobs they wanted to do on ActiveBook or on the website.

Authentic BBC interviews

www.pearsonELT.com/speakout

What can you do in English?

Now is a good time to stop and think about your learning. Look at the questionnaire. What can you do in English?

Tick the boxes for You.

		You	Your partner
1	I can count to a hundred and say the alphabet.	☐	☐
2	I can talk about my family.	☐	☐
3	I can order food and drink in a café.	☐	☐
4	I can pronounce /bægz/ and /mʌðə/.	☐	☐
5	I can ask someone about their daily routines.	☐	☐
6	I can describe my breakfast this morning.	☐	☐
7	I can tell the time.	☐	☐
8	I can talk about transport in my town.	☐	☐
9	I can buy a train ticket.	☐	☐
10	I can use correct punctuation in my writing.	☐	☐
11	I can answer questions about my last holiday.	☐	☐
12	I can use intonation to sound interested.	☐	☐
13	I can give simple directions in a shop.	☐	☐
14	I can talk about my likes and dislikes.	☐	☐
15	I can talk about my plans for next year.	☐	☐

READING AND GRAMMAR

1A Work alone and complete the questionnaire for <u>you</u>.

B Work in pairs and take turns. Complete the questionnaire for your partner.

A: Can you … ?
B: Yes, I can. How about you?
A: Yes, I think I can. Can you … ?

C Complete the sentences about you with the words in the box.

> reading   listening   speaking   writing
> grammar   pronunciation   spelling
> vocabulary

1 _____ and _____ in English are OK for me.

2 I want to improve my _____ and _____ in English.

D Work in pairs and compare your answers.

2A Read the text from a student's diary. Then replace the underlined words with the pronouns in the box.

> ~~her~~   she   we   they   me   he   us (x 2)
> them   him

Julia, my teacher, often corrects my pronunciation and so I asked ¹<u>my teacher</u> (*her*) to help ²<u>I</u>.

In the next lesson, Julia took the class to the computer room and ³<u>Julia</u> gave ⁴<u>the class</u> books.

The books were in very easy English and ⁵<u>the books</u> were all different. Then ⁶<u>the class</u> read our books and listened to ⁷<u>the books</u> on a CD. Then Julia asked ⁸<u>the class</u> to say the words with the speaker on the CD.

I think this is a good way to improve my pronunciation and my friend, Juan, said it was good for ⁹<u>Juan</u> too.

¹⁰<u>Juan</u> has problems with listening in English. He said reading and listening together was useful.

B Work in pairs and answer the questions.

1 Do you read books or magazines or websites in English? Which ones?

2 Do you read and listen to books at the same time? Why is this useful?

3 Do you sometimes listen and say the words with the speaker? Why is this useful?

115

REVIEW 5: UNITS 9–10

LISTENING AND GRAMMAR

3A ▶ R5.1 Listen to students talk about learning English. Match the speaker and the problem.

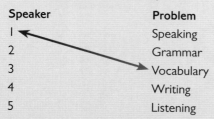

Speaker	Problem
1	Speaking
2	Grammar
3	Vocabulary
4	Writing
5	Listening

B Listen again and underline the correct alternative.

1 I'm going to learn *seven/ten* new words every day.
2 I'm going to look at the BBC news website and *read/write* down new words.
3 In the *lesson/coffee break*, I'm not going to speak in my language.
4 I'm going to listen to my CD and read the audio scripts *at the same time/sometimes*.
5 I'm going to *write/read* a diary every night, in English.
6 I'm going to write about my *life/day*.

C Which three things in Exercise 3B do you think are the best ideas?

SPEAKING

4A Work alone. Choose two learning goals from column A. Make notes about your plans in column B. Use ideas from Exercise 3A and your own ideas.

A	B
I want to improve my ...	so I'm going to ...
reading	
writing	
listening	
speaking	
vocabulary	
grammar	
pronunciation	

B Work in groups and take turns. Tell other students about your plans.

5 Work in groups. Look at page 117 and play the Speakout Game.

SOUNDS: /ɑː/ AND /ɜː/

6A ▶ R5.2 Listen to the sounds and the words. Then listen and repeat.

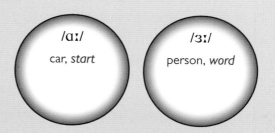

/ɑː/	/ɜː/
car	person

B ▶ R5.3 Listen and put the words in the box in the correct group. Then listen and repeat.

~~start~~ ~~word~~ first last party learn
girlfriend guitarist can't work circle dance

/ɑː/	/ɜː/
car, *start*	person, *word*

7A Work in pairs. Complete the word and circle the sound in each word.

	/ɑː/
a country	Ⓐrgentina
a fruit	b_____
a month	M_____
a form of *be*	a_____
an adjective	f_____
a time of day	a_____
a verb	l_____

	/ɜː/
a nationality	G_____
a colour	P_____
a type of clothes	s_____
a day	Th_____
a form of *be*	w_____
an adjective	th_____
a number	th_____

B Work with another pair and compare.

Work in groups and take turns. Student A: roll the dice and move your counter to the correct square. Look at the colour of the square and follow the instructions on the square in the same colour at the top.

Talk for thirty seconds about this	Say and spell three words	Make and ask the question	Say three phrases from this situation

Start	1 your town/city or country	2 transport	3 what/you/usually/do/at the weekend?	4 ordering in a café	5 your family
11 countries	10 why/you/like/speak/ English?	9 asking for information about a concert	8 a favourite object	7 places	6 what/you/do/tonight?
12 buying a train ticket	13 shopping	14 drink	15 what/you/do/last weekend?	16 telling the time	17 your daily routine
23 food	22 you/here/this time last week?	21 giving directions	20 your diet	19 adjectives for feelings	18 what/your favourite subject/in school?
24 starting a conversation	25 how you travel	26 colours	27 be/good restaurant/near here?	28 in a hotel	29 your life ten years ago
35 jobs	34 what time/you/get home/every day?	33 asking the teacher a classroom question	32 last weekend	31 clothes	30 you/happy?
36 making a request	37 your perfect job	38 office objects	39 when/you/last/travel/by boat?	40 ending a conversation	Finish!

I don't understand.

It's your turn.

What does ___ mean?

117

LANGUAGE BANK

GRAMMAR

1.1 be: I/you

Positive			
+	I	'm am	Junko. from Japan.
	You	're are	

Negative			
–	I	'm not am not	Felipa.
	You	aren't are not	from Peru. from here.

I'm = *I am*. *You're* = *You are*. Use contractions (*I'm, you're*) in speaking.

Questions			
?	Where	am	I?
		are	you	from?
	Am	I	right?
	Are	you	Ed Black? from Sydney?

I'm in classroom 3.   *Am I in classroom 3?*

You're Jim.   *Are you Jim?*

Use *be* + subject (*I/you*) for questions.

Short answers		
Yes,	I	am.
	you	are.
No,	I	'm not.
	you	aren't.

Use short answers to *yes/no* questions: *Are you David Snow? Yes, I am* ~~David Snow~~.

Don't use contractions in positive short answers: *Yes, I am.* NOT ~~Yes, I'm.~~

Use *be* with names: *I'm Olga.*

Use *be* to say or ask where a person is from: *Are you from Russia?*

Use *be* with ages: *I'm nine.*

1.2 be: he/she/it

Positive and negative			
+	He She	's is	a doctor. from Germany.
	It		in South Africa.
–	He/She/It	isn't is not	right.

He's, she's, it's = *he is, she is, it is.*

He isn't, she isn't, it isn't = *he is not, she is not, it is not.*

Use contractions (*he's, she's,* etc.) in speaking.

Questions				
?	Where	is	he/she/it	from?
		Is		in Australia?

Use *be* + subject (*he/she/it*) for questions.

She's a student.   *Is she a student?*

Short answers		
Yes,	he/she/it	is.
No,		isn't.

Use short answers to *yes/no* questions: *Is she from Spain? Yes, she is.*

Don't use contractions in positive short answers: *Yes, it is.* NOT ~~Yes, it's.~~

Use *be* + *a/an* to talk about jobs: *I'm a nurse. He's an actor.*

1.3 giving personal information

What's What is	your	first name? family name? nationality? job? phone number? email address?

I'm	Argentinian. an engineer.

It's	Marie. 0147385. marie.973@hotmail.com

For email addresses, say: *marie **dot** nine seven three **at** hotmail **dot** com.*

For telephone numbers, for *0*, say *oh* in British English. In American English, say *oh* or *zero.*

PRACTICE

1.1

A Complete the conversation with words in the box.

'm	Am	're	I	you
I'm	'm	Are	not	
I'm	aren't	you're		

A: Hi, I ¹_'m_ Wayne.

B: Hi, ²_____ 'm Jed.

A: ³_____ you from Australia?

B: ⁴_____ I from Australia?

A: Yes.

B: No, I'm ⁵_____.

A: You ⁶_____ from Australia. Really?

B: That's right. ⁷_____ from New Zealand.

A: You ⁸_____ from New Zealand! Where in New Zealand?

B: I ⁹_____ from Wellington.

A: Oh, ¹⁰_____ from Wellington, New Zealand. Nice.

B: Thanks.

A: Are ¹¹_____ OK?

B: No, ¹²_____ not!

B Put the words in the correct order. Start with the underlined word.

A: ¹ I / George / 'm / <u>Hi,</u>   _Hi, I'm George._

B: ² are / from / <u>Where</u> / you?

A: ³ 'm / Italy / from / <u>I.</u>

B: ⁴ from / <u>Are</u> / Rome / you?

A: ⁵ I'm / <u>No,</u> / not. ⁶ Venice / from / I'm.
⁷ you / from / Rome / <u>Are?</u>

B: ⁸ from / I'm / Italy / <u>No,</u> / not.
⁹ Barcelona, / I'm / Spain / from / in.

1.2

A Complete the answers.

1 Where's Kuala Lumpur?
It / Malaysia. _____It's in Malaysia_____.

2 Where's Edinburgh?
It / Scotland. _____.

3 Where's Roger Federer from?
He / Switzerland. _____.

4 Is Angela Merkel from Germany?
Yes, / she. _____.

5 Is Hyundai from Japan?
No, / it. It / South Korea. _____.

6 Where's the Maracanã Stadium?
It / Brazil. _____.

7 Is Emma Watson from the US?
No, / she. She / England. _____.

8 Is Buenos Aires in Brazil?
No, / it. It / Argentina. _____.

B Complete the questions.

1 __Where's__ Frank?
He's in New York.

2 _____ Maria _____?
She's from Portugal.

3 _____ Auckland _____ Australia?
No, it isn't. It's in New Zealand.

4 _____ Dublin?
It's in Ireland.

5 _____ waiter?
No, he's a customer.

6 _____ teacher?
No, she's a student.

7 _____ from Germany?
Yes, it is.

8 _____ Magda?
She's in Warsaw.

1.3

A Find and correct the mistakes in the conversation. There are six mistakes.

A: What ⟨'s⟩ your first name?

B: Ana.

A: And what's your family name?

B: I'm Fernandez.

A: What's you nationality?

B: I'm Italian.

A: And your number phone?

B: It's 0372 952 594.

A: What's email address?

B: It's anastella247@hotmail.com.

A: How you spell 'anastella'? With one 'n'?

B: Yes, one 'n' and two 'l's.

2.1 be: you/we/they

Positive and negative			
+	You	're	students
	We	are	from India.
–	They	aren't	married.*
		are not	

Questions and short answers				
?	Where	are	you/we/they	from?
		Are		in the right room?
	Yes,		you/we/they	are.
	No,			aren't.

*married = husband and wife

Use *you* for one person or for two, three, four, etc. people.

you   *you*

They're married.   Are they married?

Use *be* + subject (*you/ we/ they*) for questions.

Use short answers to yes/no questions: *Are you students?*
Yes, we are. NOT ~~Yes, we're students~~.

Don't use contractions in positive short answers:
Yes, they are. NOT *Yes,* ~~they're~~.

2.2 possessive adjectives: my/your/his/her/its/our/their

subject pronoun	possessive adjective
I	my
you	your
he	his
she	her
it	its
we	our
they	their

Use *your pens*, NOT ~~yours~~ pens.

Use *its* for things and animals.

Look at the spelling:

It's = it is. *It's a cat.*

Its = possessive: *Its name is Lucky.* NOT ~~It's~~ *name is Lucky.*

My name's Paolo.

Its name's Lucky.

His name's Rob.

Our family name's Romano.

Her name's Ana.

Their names are Sarah and Nick.

2.3 making suggestions

suggestions		response
Let's (Let us)	go. stop. eat.	Good idea. OK. Great.
Let's not	have a coffee. have a break. sit down.	

Use *let's* + verb to suggest a good idea.

It is a suggestion for you and me.

The negative is *Let's not* + verb: *Let's not go.*

PRACTICE

2.1

A Change the words in bold to *they*, *we* or *you*.

1 Kevin and Nick are actors.
   They're actors.

2 Michelle and I are from France.
   _____.

3 You and Chan are in the wrong room.
   _____.

4 Are your mother and father Brazilian?
   _____?

5 My teachers are Louise and Kerri.
   _____.

6 Ryan and I are married.
   _____.

7 The students aren't in class.
   _____.

8 A: Where are you and Jeff?
   _____?

   B: Jeff and I are in class.
   _____.

B Complete the conversation.

A: Hi, where / you / from?
_____?

B: We / California.
_____.

A: you / Los Angeles?
_____?

B: No / we / not. We / San Francisco.
_____.

A: you / Kathy and Chris?
_____?

B: No, / they / in Room 205!
_____.

2.2

A Complete the sentences with the words in the box.

| my our its her their his your (x 2) |

   my
1 A: Hi, ⌐name's Gina. What's name?
   B: Hi, I'm Brad.
2 A: Who's she?
   B: Oh, name's Julia.
3 A: And who's the man with Julia?
   B: I don't know name.
4 A: It's an American sport.
   B: What's name?
   A: American football!
5 A: Mr and Mrs Black, what's phone number?
   B: phone number's 2048 306 8420473.
6 A: This is a photo of the children.
   B: What are names?
   A: Jake and Patsy.

B Complete the conversations with the correct subject pronoun (*I/ you/ he*, etc.) or correct possessive adjective (*my/ your/ his*, etc.).

Conversation 1
A: Excuse me, is [1]_____ name Black?
B: No, [2]_____ isn't. [3]_____ name's Depp.
A: Are [4]_____ Johnny Depp, the actor?
B: No, [5]_____ 'm not! Please go away!

Conversation 2
A: Where's Angela?
B: [6]_____ isn't here.
A: What's [7]_____ mobile number?
B: Sorry, I don't know.

Conversation 3
A: Are [8]_____ students?
B: Yes, [9]_____ are. Are you [10]_____ teacher?
A: Yes, [11]_____ am.

2.3

A Find and correct the mistakes. There are three mistakes in each conversation.

Conversation 1
A: I'm very tired.
B: OK, ~~let~~ stop now. *let's*
A: That a good idea.
B: And let's a coffee.
A: No, thanks. I'm not thirsty.

Conversation 2
A: I hungry.
B: I too.
A: Let we eat at the pizzeria.
B: Good idea.

3.1 *this/that/these/those*

	here ↓	there ↘
singular	this key	that key
plural	these keys	those keys

With *this/that*, use *is*: This **is** my book. That**'s** your book.

With *these/those*, use *are*: These **are** my DVDs. Those **are** your DVDs.

this *that*

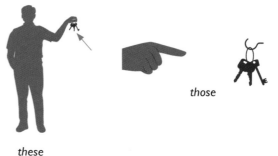

these *those*

3.2 possessive *'s*

He's	my father's	brother.
They're	my friend's	children.
They're	Rob's	keys.
Is that	Francis's	mobile?
Mariam is	Jalil and Laila's	daughter.
	Catherine's	family name is Hart.

Use *'s* to show possession.

Use *'s* with objects: *Rebecca's car, Wei's book.*

Use *'s* with personal information:
James's email address, Lorenzo's phone number.

Use *'s* with family: *Eva's parents, Lucy's brother.*

With two people, put the *'s* after the second person: *That is Carl and Olga's house.*

Note: <u>Tony's</u> *a waiter* = Tony is.

     I'm <u>Tony's</u> *father* = possessive *'s*.

Use *'s* after a word ending in s: *I like Boris's coat.*

3.3 ordering in a café

Ordering			
Can I have	a	tea, mineral water, cake,	please?
	two	coffees, colas, sandwiches,	
How much is that?			

Taking orders
Can I help you?
Anything else?
That's £8.

giving alternatives			response
Still		sparkling?	Still, please.
White	or	brown bread?	Brown, please.
Espresso		cappucino?	Espresso, please.

PRACTICE

3.1

A Look at the picture and complete the conversation with *this, that, these* or *those*.

A: Excuse me, is ¹ *this* your shop?

B: Yes, it is.

A: And is ² _____ your window?

B: Yes. Is ³ _____ your football?

A: No, it's their football.

B: Are ⁴ _____ your children?

A: Yes, ⁵ _____'s Jerry and ⁶ _____'s Ed.

B Find and correct the mistakes with *this/that/these/those* in the conversations.

Conversation 1

    These
A: ~~This~~ are our photos of Thailand.

B: Is this your hotel?

A: Yes, it is, and this are our friends, Sanan and Chai.

Conversation 2

A: What's this over there?

B: It's Red Square. And this is your hotel here.

A: Thank you.

Conversation 3

A: What are those in English?

B: They're 'coins'. That one here is a pound coin.

Conversation 4

A: Who are that people over there?

B: That's my brother, Juan and his friends.

Conversation 5

A: Where are those students from?

B: They're from Bogotá, in Colombia.

A: And those student?

B: She isn't a student. She's our teacher!

3.2

A Write sentences about the family. Use possessive *'s.*

Jon and Ellen

Mark   **Sarah**

1 Jon is *Ellen's* husband.

2 Ellen is _____ mother.

3 Mark is _____ brother.

4 Sarah is _____ sister.

5 Mark is _____ son.

6 Sarah is _____ daughter.

7 Ellen is _____ wife.

8 Jon and Ellen are _____ parents.

B Complete the sentences with possessive *'s.*

1 He's Matt. This is his computer.

  This is _Matt's computer_ .

2 That's Josh. I'm his friend.

  I'm _____.

3 She's Emily. Are you her sister?

  Are you _____?

4 He's Eric. His family name's White.

  Eric _____'s White.

5 They're Bella and David. These are their children.

  These are _____ children.

6 This is Rex. His phone number is 396 294.

  _____ is 396 294.

3.3

A Complete the conversation with the words in the box.

~~you~~   that's   have   or   one   can   else

    you
A: Can I help ⌄ ?

B: Yes, can I an egg sandwich, please?

A: White brown bread?

B: Brown, please.

A: Anything?

B: Yes, I have two coffees, please?

A: Espresso or cappuccino?

B: One espresso and cappuccino.

A: OK, six fifty.

4 LANGUAGE BANK

GRAMMAR

4.1 present simple: I/you/we/they

Positive and negative			
+	I	work	in an office.
	You	have	two children.
–	We	don't like	egg sandwiches.
	They	do not like	

For the negative, use *don't* + verb: *I don't live here. Don't = do not.* Use the contraction *don't* in speaking.

Use the present simple to talk about things that are always true.

Questions					Short answers		
?	Do	you/we/they	have	a car?	Yes,	I /we/they	do.
					No,		don't.

For a question, use *do* + subject + verb. *Do you understand?* NOT ~~understand you?~~

In short answers, use *Yes, I do. No, I don't.* NOT ~~Yes, I understand. No, I don't understand~~.

Wh- questions			
Where	do	you	live?
What			study?
When			

Use a question word (*what, where*) + do + subject + verb: *Where do you work?*

4.2 present simple: he/she/it

Positive and negative			
+	He	likes	children.
	She	goes	to Mexico.
	It	has	an airport.
–	He	doesn't live	in Barcelona.
	She	does not work	in a bank.
	It	doesn't have	a market.

For the negative, use *doesn't* + verb: *She doesn't like chocolate.*
Doesn't = does not. Use the contraction *doesn't* in speaking.

Spelling rules: present simple: *he/she/it*		
verbs type:	rule	example
	+ -s	work – he works / love – she loves
verbs ending in:		
-ch, -o, -s, -sh, -x	+ -es	teach – he teaches / do – she does
consonant + -y	y + -ies	study – he studies / cry – she cries

Have is irregular: *He has a new computer.*

4.3 telling the time

Asking the time
What time is it?
What time is the film/match/lesson?

Telling the time
It's two o'clock.
The match is at three o'clock.

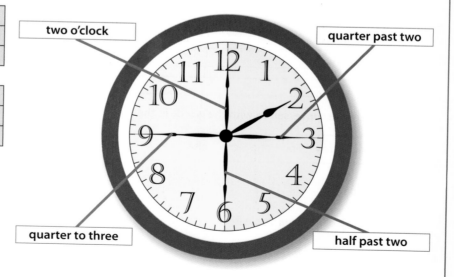

two o'clock / quarter past two / quarter to three / half past two

PRACTICE

4.1

A Complete the sentences with the verbs in the box.

| read write eat have know drive like live |

1 I ___don't read___ newspapers (−)
2 You _____ the colour red. (+)
3 They _____ a sister. (−)
4 We _____ to work. (−)
5 I _____ emails in English. (+)
6 We _____ in Rome. (+)
7 They _____ a lot of cakes! (+)
8 You _____ the answer. (−)

B Put the words in the correct order to make questions.

1 like / Do / children / you?
   Do you like children?
2 and / live / you / Jack / together / Do?
3 you / in / work / Do / an / office?
4 sweater / Do / have / black / you / a?
5 Do / Spanish / understand / parents / your?
6 work / to / walk / you / Do ?

C Complete the short answers for questions 1–6 in Exercise B.

1 Yes, ___I do___.
2 No, _____.
3 Yes, _____.
4 No, _____.
5 Yes, _____.
6 No, _____.

D Write the questions. Use the words in bold to help.

1 _____*What do you study?*_____ (you)
   I study **English**.
2 _____? (you)
   We work in **Hong Kong**.
3 _____? (we)
   You have a break **at ten**.
4 _____? (you)
   G-e-o-r-g-e.
5 _____? (they)
   They like **sport and TV**.

4.2

A Complete the sentences with the correct form of the verbs in brackets.

1 My mother ___lives___ in Paris because she ___likes___ cities. (live, like)
2 Rudy _____ me but he _____ me every week. (not email, phone)
3 My husband _____ to work or he _____. (drive, walk)
4 Lana _____ at home but she _____ it. (work, not like)
5 Marco _____ four coffees every day because _____ tea. (have, not like)
6 Gina _____ English but she _____ it. (understand, not speak)

B Find and correct three mistakes in each conversation.

Conversation 1

A: My wife, Kalila, is a teacher.
B: Near here?
A: Yes, she have a job at City School. She teachs Arabic.
B: Is it a good place to work?
A: Yes, but she don't like the travel every day.

Conversation 2

A: My son Jaime studys engineering at Madrid University.
B: Oh, my daughter gos there. She likes it a lot.
A: Yes, Jaime sais it's good too.

4.3

A Write the times in words.

1 _____
2 _____
3 _____
4 _____
5 _____
6 _____
7 _____
8 _____

1	2	3	4
5:00	6:15	9:30	8:45

5	6	7	8
4:45	12:30	11:00	7:15

5.1 present simple questions: *he/she/it*

Yes/No questions:				
?	Does	he / she / it	have	a big breakfast?

Short answers		
Yes,	he / she / it	does.
No,		doesn't.

Use *does* + subject + verb for a question. *Does she cook dinner?* NOT ~~cooks she dinner?~~

In short answers, use *Yes, he does. No, he doesn't.* NOT ~~Yes, she cooks. No, she doesn't cook.~~

Wh- questions				
?	When	does	he / she / it	get up?
	What time			have breakfast?
	Where			live?
	What			do?

Use a question word (*what, where, what time, when*) + *does* + subject + verb: *When does she eat?*

5.2 adverbs of frequency

Positive and negative				
+	I/You/We	always usually often sometimes never	work	on Sundays.
	He/She		has	a coffee.
–	I/You/We	don't usually	cook	breakfast.
	He/She	doesn't often	have	

Adverbs of frequency go **before** most verbs. *I **sometimes** write emails in English.*

Adverbs of frequency with *be*				
+	I	'm	always	hungry.
	It	's	usually	here.
–	She	isn't	often	

Adverbs of frequency go **after** the verb *be*. *I'm **often** tired.*

Use adverbs of frequency to say how often we do activities. *I always do my homework. He doesn't often play tennis.*

never	not often	sometimes	often	usually	always
0%	10%	40%	60%	80%	100%

5.3 asking for information

Questions			
What time When	does	the tour	leave?
		the café	open?
	is	lunch?	
How much	does	it	cost?
	is	it?	

Responses	
It opens	at nine.
	from 6a.m. to 10p.m.
	every day except Monday.
It closes	at two o'clock.
It leaves	at half past nine.
It costs It's	twenty euros.

PRACTICE

5.1

A Put the words in the correct order to make questions.

1 live / Does / here / Patrizia?
   Does Patrizia live here?
2 Chinese / Stefan / Does / speak?
3 Katia / Does / children / have?
4 your / like / job / brother / his / Does?
5 a / cat / have / Does / name / your?
6 word / this / Does / mean / 'very big'?

B Complete the answers with *does* or *doesn't*.

a) Yes, she ___does___. A son and a daughter.
b) Yes, she _____. In flat five.
c) No, it _____. It means 'very good'.
d) Yes, he _____, but he works from eight to seven.
e) No, he _____, but he speaks Japanese.
f) Yes, it _____. Its name is Fluffy.

C Match questions 1–6 with answers a)–f).

1b)

D Complete the questions. Use the words in brackets.

Conversation 1
A: Where ¹*does your brother live?* (your brother)
B: He lives in Copenhagen.
A: Where ² _____?(he)
B: He works in a school.

Conversation 2
A: What time ³ _____? (Cristina)
B: She gets home at half past four.
A: And when ⁴ _____? (she)
B: She has dinner at six o'clock.

Conversation 3
A: What ⁵ _____? ('late')
B: It means after the correct time.
A: Oh. And what time ⁶ _____?
   (the lesson)
B: It starts at 9a.m.

5.2

A Complete the sentences. Use the words in brackets.

1 I do sport. (never)
   I never do sport.
2 My mother phones me on Monday evenings. (usually)
3 He's tired in the mornings. (often)
4 We have a drink after work on Fridays. (always)
5 Do you walk to work? (usually)
6 I'm at home in the afternoons. (not usually)
7 Classes are on Saturdays. (sometimes)
8 I watch TV. (not often)

B Look at the chart and complete the conversation. Use adverbs of frequency.

	Mon	Tue	Wed	Thu	Fri	Sat	Sun
vegetables							
fruit							✔
chicken	✔		✔		✔	✔	
steak	✔	✔	✔	✔	✔	✔	✔
fish		✔		✔			
chips	✔	✔	✔		✔	✔	✔

A: So, Mr Price, let's look at your diet. Do you eat vegetables and fruit?
B: Er, no, doctor. I _never_ _eat_ vegetables and I _____ _____ _____ fruit.
A: What about meat and fish?
B: Well, I _____ _____ fish, maybe once or twice a week and I _____ _____ chicken. I like steak so I _____ _____ steak for lunch and I _____ _____ it with chips.

5.3

A Complete the conversation with the words in the box.

| ~~me~~ do to it does what opens except |

A: Excuse *me* ?
B: Can I help you?
A: Yes, time is dinner?
B: From seven half past ten.

A: And you have a swimming pool?
B: Yes, it opens every day Sunday.
A: When does open?
B: It at seven in the morning.
A: When it close?
B: I closes at nine in the evening.

6.1 there is/are

Positive and negative				
+	There	's	a restaurant	in the station.
		is	a snack bar	here.
		are	payphones	near here.
−	There	isn't	a hotel	over there.
		aren't	any cafés	

Questions			Short answers		
Is	there	a cash machine here?	Yes,	there	is.
			No,		isn't.
Are	there	any shops in the station?	Yes	there	are.
			No,		aren't.

There's a pharmacy.   *Is there a pharmacy?*

Use short answers to *yes/no* questions: *Is there a café? Yes, there is?* NOT ~~Yes, there is a café.~~

Use *Is there a/an* + noun / *Are* + *there* + (*any*) + plural noun for *yes/no* questions.

With plural nouns, use *any* in the question form and the negative.

*Are there **any** shops? There aren't **any** shops.*

Use *there's* (*there is*) and *there are* to say something exists.

Use *there's* (*there is*) and *there are* to talk about places, and things or people in places.

6.2 a/an, some, a lot of, not any

a/an

some

a lot of   not any

Use *a/an* + singular noun for one thing or person. Use *a* before consonants (*b, c, d, f,* etc.) and *an* before vowels (*a, e, i, o, u*).

*There's **a** problem. Can I have **an egg** sandwich?*

Use *some* + plural noun for a small number of things or people.

*I have **some stamps** in my bag.*

Use *a lot of* + plural noun for a large number of things or people.

*Are there **a lot of students** in your class?*

Use *not any* + plural noun for zero (0).

*I don't have **any bananas**.*

*There aren't **any buses**.*

Also use *no* + noun for zero.

*I have **no bananas**. There are **no buses**.*

6.3 buying a ticket

Asking for a ticket	
A single	to Cairo, please.
A return	to Paris for tomorrow, please.
Two singles	
A monthly pass	to Victoria Station, please.

Asking for information		
What time	's	the next bus?
When	is	
	does it arrive	in Dublin?

Giving information		
What time	do you want	to go?
When		to come back?
There's	a bus	at half past four.
	one	
The train	leaves from	platform 2.
The bus		gate 21.

PRACTICE

6.1

A Look at the picture and read the sentences. Write sentences beginning with *There's*, *There are*, *There isn't* or *There aren't*.

1 *There's a book*, so I think the woman likes reading.
2 _____, so I think she likes the cinema.
3 _____, so she works in a bank.
4 _____, so she doesn't have a car.
5 _____, so she's married.
6 _____, so she doesn't have good eyes.
7 _____, so she likes cats.
8 _____, so maybe she doesn't have any children.

B Complete the conversations with the words in the box.

| ~~Is there~~   aren't   there (x 2)   are (x 3) |
| there's   isn't   Are   is (x 2) |

Conversation 1

A: ¹ *Is there* a wallet on the table?

B: No, there ²_____, but ³_____ a bag.

Conversation 2

A: Excuse me, ⁴_____ ⁵_____ any toilets near here?

B: Yes, there ⁶_____ men's and women's toilets over there.

Conversation 3

A: ⁷_____ there any night buses?

B: No, there ⁸_____, but there ⁹_____ taxis.

Conversation 4

A: Excuse me, ¹⁰_____ ¹¹_____ a doctor here?

B: Yes, there ¹²_____. Dr Mantel!

6.2

A Look at the picture and complete the sentences with *There's/are* and *a/an, some, a lot of* or *n't (not) any*.

1 _____ *There's a* _____ phone.
2 _____ photos.
3 _____ computer.
4 _____ apple.
5 _____ pens.
6 _____ keys.

B Put the words in order to make sentences.

1 have / lot / money / Students / a / of / don't
2 a / pages / has / lot / book / A / usually / of
3 have / Some / don't / people / home / a
4 any / but / sister / Ben / have / has / brothers / he / doesn't / a
5 of / Our / has / lot / students / school / a
6 a / of / Some / have / lot / children / people

6.3

A Complete the conversation with the words in the box.

| ~~singles~~   a   's   do   it   tomorrow |

singles
A: Two ⌄ to Glasgow, please.
B: For today?
A: Sorry, no, for.
B: When you want to go?
A: At about nine o'clock in the morning.
B: OK, that's seven pounds fifty.
A: What time the bus?
B: There's one at quarter to nine.
A: When does arrive in Glasgow?
B: At half past nine.
A: Thanks lot.

7.1 past simple: was/were

Positive and negative				
+	I/He/She/It	was	here	yesterday.
	You/We/They	were	at work	on Friday.
–	I/He/She/It	wasn't	tired	this morning.
	You/We/They	weren't		

The past simple of *be* is *was/were*. Use *was/were* to talk about the past.

Add *n't* (*not*) for the negative: *wasn't = was not*, *weren't = were not*.

Use contractions in speaking: *I wasn't here yesterday.*

Wh- questions with *was/were*		
Where	was	your party?
When	were	the last Olympic Games?

Use *Wh-* question words + *was/were* + subject to ask questions in the past.

What was the problem?

Questions				Short answers		
?	Was	I/he/she/it	OK? right?	Yes,	I/he/she/it	was.
				No,		wasn't.
	Were	you/we/they	here	Yes	you/we/they	were.
				No,		weren't.

Use *was/were* + subject (*I, you*) for questions.

She was in Spain. → *Was she in Spain?*
You were at school together. → *Were you at school together?*

Use short answers to *yes/no* questions:
Was it good? Yes, it was. NOT Yes, it was ~~good~~.

7.2 past simple: regular verbs

Positive and negative			
+	I/You/He/She/It/We/They	worked	yesterday.
		closed	at four.
		cried	all night.
		stopped	last week.
–		didn't wait.	
		did not start.	

Spellings: regular past simple verbs		
types of verb	rule	example
verbs ending in:		
	+ -ed	work – worked
-e	+ -d	close – closed
consonant + -y	y + -ied	cry – cried
consonant-vowel-consonant	double the final consonant + -ed	stop – stopped

Note: opened, listened NOT ~~openned, listenned~~

The past simple is the same for *I/You/He/She/It/We/They.*

In the negative, use *didn't* + verb. *I didn't dance.* NOT *I ~~didn't danced~~.*

Use the contraction *didn't* in speaking.

Use the past simple to talk about:
• something which happened at a point in the past.
*We **arrived** at three o'clock.*

• something which started and finished in the past.
*We **played** tennis for three hours.*

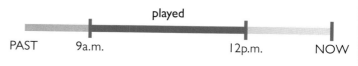

7.3 giving opinions

Asking for opinions		
How	is	the food?
	was	the party?

Giving opinions		
It	is/was	delicious.
		lovely.
They	're/were	great.
		fantastic.
		good.
		boring.
It	wasn't	very good.

Use *I think* with opinions: *I think it's very good.*

PRACTICE

7.1

A Complete the sentences with the correct form of *be* in the present or the past.

1 I ___'m___ (+) here now but I _wasn't_ (–) here yesterday.

2 He _____ (–) at home today, but he _____ (+) at home yesterday.

3 The shops _____ (–) open yesterday, but they _____ (+) open today.

4 We _____ (+) all tired yesterday, but we _____ (–) tired today.

5 She _____ (–) at work yesterday, but she _____ (+) at work today.

6 You _____ (+) relaxed today, but you _____ (–) relaxed yesterday.

B Complete the questions about the past and write the short answers.

1 James / here / this morning? ✗
   Was James here this morning? _No, he wasn't._

2 the film / good? ✓
   _____? _____.

3 your brothers and sisters / nice to you? ✓
   _____? _____.

4 you / cold / in Scotland? ✗
   _____? _____.

5 you and Emma / at the party? ✗
   _____? _____.

6 there / a gift shop / in the hotel? ✓
   _____? _____.

7.2

A Write the sentences in the past simple with the words in brackets.

1 The shop opens at ten. (Yesterday / nine)
   Yesterday the shop opened at nine.

2 My father plays golf at the weekend. (Last weekend / tennis)
   _____

3 Francisco works in a bank. (Last year / shop)
   _____

4 The baby cries a lot. (Last night / all night)
   _____

5 My parents often move home. (In 2009 / to Barcelona)
   _____

6 The train stops for a quarter of an hour. (Yesterday / half an hour)
   _____

B Complete the sentences with the correct form of the past simple.

1 In 2010 / we / live / in London, but / we / not / like / it.
   In 2010 we lived in London, but we didn't like it.

2 I / not / watch / TV last night. I study / for three hours.

3 Noriko / email / me yesterday, but she / not / phone.

4 The film / not / start / until eight, and / it / finish / at eleven.

5 James / want / to see the concert, but he / arrive / an hour late.

6 I / repeat / the instructions because / the students / not / understand.

7.3

A Find and correct the mistakes. There are three mistakes in each conversation.

Conversation 1

A: Hi, Sally. ^*How* ~~Who~~ was the film?

B: It was delicious, really great.

A: Who was in it?

B: Tom Hanks.

A: How is he?

B: He was fantastic.

Conversation 2

A: Who's the chicken?

B: It's very good – really awful.

A: Oh, I'm sorry.

B: How about your steak?

A: I'm think it's OK.

B: And this restaurant is very expensive.

A: Yes, it is!

8.1 past simple: irregular verbs

+	I/You/We/They/ He/She/It		went	camping.
			had	a good time.
			met	a lot of people.

−	I/You/We/They/ He/She/It	didn't	go	on holiday.
			have	breakfast.
			met	our friends.

Many common verbs have an irregular past simple form.

The negative form is the same for regular and irregular verbs.

I didn't go camping. NOT *I didn't went camping.*

He didn't have a good time. NOT *He didn't had a good time.*

8.2 past simple: questions

Yes/No questions						Short answers		
?	Did	I/you/he/she/it/ we/they	start	in New York?		Yes,	I/you/he/she/it/ we/they	did.
			go	to Paris?		No,		didn't.

Use *Did* + subject + verb for a question. *Did you start?* NOT *Did you started? Did you went?*

The question form is the same for regular and irregular verbs.

In short answers, use *Yes, I did/No, I didn't.* NOT *Yes, I started. No, I didn't go.*

Wh- questions			
When			
Where	did	you	go?
Why			
How			
What	did	you	do?
Who	did	you	meet?

The question word is before *did*.

8.3 giving directions

Asking for directions		
Excuse me,	where's	the fruit?
	where are	the DVDs?
	is there	a post office near here?

Giving directions		
Do you see	the vegetables?	
	the shop over there?	
The fruit	is	next to the vegetables.
The DVDs	are	opposite the magazines.
		on the right.
		near the yoghurts.
There	's	a post office over there.

To check instructions, use: *Let me check* or *Can I check?*

PRACTICE

8.1

A Complete the sentences with the correct form of the verb in bold.

I   They didn't **come** to class on Monday but they ___came___ on Tuesday.

2   He **took** a taxi, he didn't _____ a bus.

3   You **said** hello, but you didn't _____ your name.

4   She didn't **think** the film was good but he _____ it was great.

5   I didn't **become** a nurse, I _____ a doctor.

6   We didn't **sit** here, we _____ over there.

B Complete the story with the past form of the verbs in the box.

~~meet~~   break   drive   go   have (x 2)   give   see   become   not have   eat

I ¹___met___ my wife Manuela one weekend on a mountain in Scotland. On that Saturday morning the weather was good and I ²_____ out at eight o'clock. But around two o'clock the weather ³_____ very bad. At five o'clock I was lost, cold, very hungry and scared. Then I ⁴_____ someone on the mountain. It was Manuela. She ⁵_____ any food but she ⁶_____ some chocolate and some water. She ⁷_____ the chocolate in two and ⁸_____ me half. We ⁹_____ the chocolate and talked. Then she helped me down the mountain. She ¹⁰_____ a car and she ¹¹_____ me back to my hotel. I asked her to dinner and that was the beginning of our story.

8.2

A Complete the conversations with the past form of the verbs in brackets.

I   A: ___Did___ you ___leave___ home at six in the morning? (leave)

B: Yes, we ___did___. But the plane ___left___ at six in the evening!

2   A: _____ you _____ David at school? (meet)

B: No, I_____. We _____ last year at work.

3   A: _____ you _____ at the party? (dance)

B: Yes, I _____. I _____ with Sally, and Anne, and Julia.

4   A: _____ you _____ Mike yesterday afternoon? (see)

B: No, I _____, but I _____ him in the morning.

5   A: _____ you _____ this email? (write)

B: Yes, I _____. I _____ it yesterday. Is there a problem?

6   A: _____ you _____ a good time in Uruguay? (have)

B: Yes, we _____. We _____ a fantastic time, thanks.

B Write questions about the underlined information.

I   I met <u>an old friend</u>.

Who did you meet?

2   We went <u>to a restaurant</u>.

_____

3   We ate <u>pizza</u>.

_____

4   We drank <u>mineral water</u>.

_____

5   We saw <u>a film</u>.

_____

6   I came home <u>at midnight</u>.

_____

8.3

A Find and correct the mistakes in the conversation. There are six mistakes.

               are

A: Excuse me, where <del>is</del> the sweets?

B: Are you see the newspapers over there?

A: Where?

B: Over there, near of the snacks.

A: Oh, yes.

B: Well, the sweets are next the newspapers, on the right.

A: Can I check? They're the left of the newspapers.

B: No, they're on right.

A: Ah, yes. Thanks a lot.

B: No problem.

9.1 like, love, hate + -ing

Positive and negative			
+	I/You/We/They	like/love/hate	cats.
	He/She/It	likes/loves/hates	computer games.
−	I/You/We/They	don't like	going to parties.
	He/She/It	doesn't like	doing nothing.

Be careful with the short answers:

Do you like playing tennis? Yes I do. NOT ~~Yes, I like.~~

No, I don't. NOT ~~No, I don't like.~~

To talk about your feelings:
- use *love/(don't) like/hate* + plural noun.
- use *love/(don't) like/hate* + verb + *-ing*.

Spellings: *-ing* forms		
type of verb	rule	example
most verbs	+ *-ing*	go – going / study – studying
verbs ending in:		
-e	e- + *-ing*	phone – phoning / drive – driving
consonant-vowel-consonant	double the final consonant + *-ing*	get – getting / sit – sitting

9.2 object pronouns

subject pronouns	object pronouns
I	me
you	you
he	him
she	her
it	it
we	us
they	them

Don't repeat nouns and noun phrases. Use a pronoun:

*Megan's brother is a doctor and I like ~~Megan's brother~~ **him** very much.*

A: *Do you know Amelia?*

B: *No, I don't know ~~Amelia~~ **her**.*

After prepositions, use nouns or object pronouns.

*Listen **to** the teacher/**to** me.*

*I went to the cinema **with** friends/**with** them.*

Subject pronouns go **before** the verb.

Object pronouns go **after** the verb.

*Karen loves cats but **I** hate **them**.*

9.3 making requests

I/He/She etc.	'd like	two coffees, please.
	would like	a new computer.

Would like is polite.

Use *would like* + noun = I want.

Note: *I'd like a banana* = I want a banana now.

I like bananas = I always like bananas.

question					response
	Would	you	like	a drink?	Yes, please. No, thanks/thank you.
What Which one	would	you	like?		I'd like a cola, please.

For questions, use *Would + you + like* (+ noun)?

Or use *Wh-* question word + *would + you + like*?

For the answer, use: *Would you like (a sandwich)?* with *Yes, please.* or *No, thanks/thank you.*

PRACTICE

9.1

A Write the -ing form of the verbs.

1. be _____being_____
2. chat _____
3. work _____
4. write _____
5. say _____
6. have _____
7. start _____
8. stop _____
9. cook _____
10. email _____

B Complete the conversations.

Conversation 1

A: you / like / do / sport? *Do you like doing sport?*

B: Well, / like / swim / but I / not / like / run.

A: you / like / play / tennis?

B: Yes, / I.

Conversation 2

A: Sam / not / like / speak / on the phone.

B: he / like / write / emails?

A: No, he / but / he / love / meet / people / online.

B: And / he / like / play / computer games?

A: Yes, / he.

9.2

A Find and correct the mistakes in the sentences. There are mistakes in eight of the sentences.

1. Leo and Irena were here yesterday. I had lunch with ~~her~~. *them*
2. That's your sister's toy. Give it to him.
3. Deena lived with we for three years.
4. I love this music. Come and dance with I.
5. I spoke to Muhammed last night and asked him about it.
6. These apples aren't very good. I don't like these.
7. When did I first talk to you?
8. Andy's good at tennis. I played with he yesterday.
9. Diana's in my class. I like she a lot.
10. The exit is over there, in front of your.

B Look at the conversations. Complete B's part with an object pronoun.

1. A: Did you see John yesterday?
   B: Yes I saw ⎡*him* at lunch.
2. A: How was the chicken?
   B: I didn't like.
3. A: Do you have the tickets?
   B: Oh, no! I put in my other coat.
4. A: You're very late!
   B: Sorry, I sent you a text. Did you get?
5. A: Where's Alex?
   B: He phoned this morning from home. He isn't well.
6. A: Was Jennifer at the party?
   B: No, I asked but she didn't want to go.
7. A: How did you and Al get to your hotel?
   B: A taxi met at the airport.
8. A: Thank you Mr Abaasi.
   B: Wait a minute, class. Did I give your homework?

9.3

A Complete the conversations with the words in the box.

| ~~Can~~ | like | Do | thanks | I'd | have | Would | 'd |

Conversation 1

A: ¹ _Can_ I help you?

B: Yes, please. I ² _____ like one of those shirts.

B: OK. Which colour would you ³ _____ ?

A: Um ... Can I ⁴ _____ the red one, please?

Conversation 2

A: ⁵ _____ you like something to drink?

B: Er ... Yes, ⁶ _____ like a tea please.

A: ⁷ _____ you take sugar?

B: No, ⁸ _____ .

10.1 *can/can't*

Positive and negative			
+	I/You/He/She/It/We/They	can	swim.
−		can't	play tennis.

Questions			Short answers		
Can	I/you/he/she/it/we/they	drive?	Yes,	I/he/she/ it/ we/they	can.
		cook Mexican food?	No,		can't.

Use *can/can't* + verb. *I can dance.* NOT ~~I can to dance~~.

Use short answers to *yes/no* questions: *Can you sing? Yes, I can./No, I can't.*

NOT ~~Yes, I can swim./No, I can't swim.~~

Use *can* + subject (*you, he*) for questions.

He can play tennis. Can he play tennis?

Use *can* or *can't* to talk about ability. You know how to do something.

Use *very well, well, quite well, not very well* with *can*.

I can speak English very well. (✓✓✓)
I can sing well. (✓✓)
I can cook quite well. (✓)
I can speak English, but not very well. (✗)

10.2 *be going to*

Positive and negative				
+	I	'm	going to	get fit.
	He/She/It	's		
	You/We/They	're		
−	I	'm not		lose weight
	He/She/It	isn't		
	You/We/They	aren't		

Use *be going to* + verb to talk about future plans.

Yes, I'm going to lose weight. But not today!.

lose weight

PAST   NOW   FUTURE

10.3 starting and ending conversations

Starting conversations
Hi, how are you?
This is a great/nice place.
Excuse me, do you have the time?
What do you think of the music/food/party?
So are you from around here?
So, where are you going?*

Ending conversations
Is that the time?
I'm sorry, I have a lesson at two.
Oh look, this is my station.
I'm sorry. I can see an old friend over there.
Nice to talk to you/meet you.
I hope we meet again.

*Use this when you meet someone on a bus, train, plane, etc.

PRACTICE

10.1

A Complete the sentences with the verb in brackets and the correct form of *can*.

1 Help, help! _____I can't swim_____! (swim)
2 Excuse me, _____ English? (speak)
3 Martin _____ a horse, but not very well. (ride)
4 I'm sorry. I _____ your name. (remember)
5 Rita _____ very good photos so let's ask her. (take)
6 These words are very small. _____ them for me? (read)
7 I _____ the game of chess. (never understand)
8 I don't have my glasses with me so I _____ very well. (see)

B Complete the conversation with *can* (x 5) and *can't* (x 4).

A: Are you OK? ⌐Can⌐ you stand up?

B: Let me try. Yes, I.

A: you walk on it?

B: I don't know. Oh no, I.

A: OK, just sit down and relax.

B: I relax! Where's my mobile?

A: I see it. You use my mobile.

B: It's no good.

A: What's the problem?

B: I get a phone signal here. you go and get help?

A: Yes, no problem. Don't move!

10.2

A Find and correct the mistakes in the sentences 1–8. There are mistakes in six of the sentences.

1 I ⌐am⌐ going to see Juan this afternoon.
2 Charlotte's going be a writer.
3 I are going to stay at home tomorrow.
4 We aren't going to arrive before seven o'clock.
5 Antonio going to leave work at five.
6 I not going to pay!
7 Kiera and Sam is going to drive to Chicago.
8 My daughter isn't going to sell her flat.

B Complete the conversation with the words in the box. You do not need to use one of the words.

| ⌐'m⌐ not buy 're go to 's he going |

A: I ¹ _'m_ going to get up early tomorrow and go running. Do you want to come?

B: No, I'm going ² _____ stay up late tonight, so I'm ³ _____ going to get up early tomorrow.

A: Oh, is there something good on TV?

B: No, it's my father's fiftieth birthday and ⁴ _____ 's going to have a party.

A: Oh, that's right. You ⁵ _____ going to give him a new mobile phone.

B: No, I'm going to ⁶ _____ him a GPS for his car. Do you want to come and help me choose one?

A: Sorry, I can't. Celia's here. She ⁷ _____ going to help me with my computer.

B: OK. I'm ⁸ _____ to go to the shop now. See you later.

10.3

A Put the words in bold in the correct order.

Conversation 1

A: Excuse me, ¹**the / you / time / do / have**? *Do you have the time?*

B: Yes, it's half past eight.

A: ²**nice / is / place / a / This.**

B: It's OK. ³**you / What / of / music / do / think / the?**

A: It's great.

Conversation 2

A: I'm sorry, ⁴**old / there / friend / can / see / an / over / I.**

B: Oh, right.

A: ⁵**you / talk / to / Nice / to.**

B: ⁶**too / talk / to / Good / you / to.**

Conversation 3

A: ⁷**that / time / Is / the?** Oh, no!

B: What's the problem?

A: ⁸**minutes / meeting / in / ten / a / have / I.**

B: OK. Goodbye.

A: Bye.

PHOTO BANK

INTERNATIONAL ENGLISH

1A Match the words with photos A–N.

1 bank
2 camera
3 cinema
4 computer
5 email
6 information
7 internet
8 pizza
9 restaurant
10 supermarket
11 taxi
12 television/TV
13 tennis
14 university

B Are the words the same in your language?

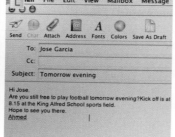

CLASSROOM LANGUAGE

1 Match the verbs with pictures A–L.

1 answer
2 ask
3 listen
4 read
5 write
6 look
7 circle
8 tick
9 underline
10 work alone
11 work in pairs
12 check your answers

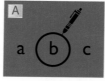
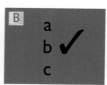

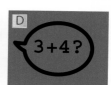

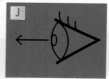

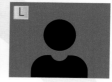

COUNTRIES AND NATIONALITIES

1A Match the countries with the flags.

1 Canada *A*
2 Egypt
3 France
4 Germany
5 Greece
6 India
7 Mexico
8 New Zealand
9 Portugal
10 Scotland
11 South Korea
12 Venezuela

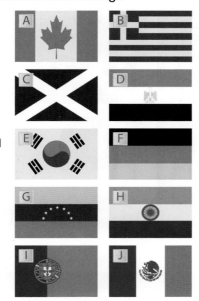

B Complete the table with the correct countries.

Nationality	Country	Nationality	Country
-an/-ian		*-ese*	
1 American		17 Chinese	
2 Argentinian		18 Japanese	
3 Australian		19 Portuguese	
4 Brazilian		*-ish*	
5 Canadian		20 English	
6 Egyptian		21 Irish	
7 German		22 Polish	
8 Hungarian		23 Scottish	
9 Indian		24 Spanish	
10 Italian		other	
11 Korean		25 French	
12 Mexican		26 Greek	
13 Russian		27 New Zealander	
14 Saudi Arabian			
15 South African			
16 Venezuelan			

JOBS

1A Match the jobs with photos A–N.

1 cleaner
2 cook/chef
3 hairdresser
4 hotel manager
5 IT worker
6 musician
7 office worker *A*
8 personal assistant
9 pilot
10 police officer
11 receptionist
12 retired
13 shop assistant
14 tourist information assistant

B Put the jobs in the correct group.

~~sportsman~~ actor businesswoman waitress actress waiter sportswoman businessman

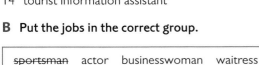
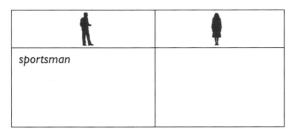

sportsman	

PHOTO BANK

FEELINGS

1A Match the adjectives with photos A–H.

1 angry
2 happy
3 ill
4 interested
5 scared/afraid
6 surprised
7 unhappy
8 well/fine

B Are the adjectives good (+) or bad (−)? Complete the table.

+	−
happy	

OBJECTS

1A Match the names of the objects with photos A–L.

1 bag
2 credit card
3 cup
4 diary
5 dictionary
6 glass
7 mouse
8 newspaper
9 notebook
10 pencil
11 table
12 watch

B Work in pairs. Which objects are in the classroom?

2A Write the plurals of the words in Exercise 1A in the correct place.

			pens
most words	+ -s	key – keys	
after -x, -ss, -sh, -ch	+ -es	box – boxes	
after consonant + -y	y + ies	city – cities	

A boy

B _____

C _____

D _____

E _____

F _____

B Write the words in the box under the photos.

~~boy~~ man children girls boys woman girl men child women

G _____

H _____

I _____

J _____

PB

CLOTHES AND COLOURS

1 Match the names of the clothes with photos A–S.

1 boots 8 jacket 15 sweater
2 coat 9 jeans 16 tie
3 dress 10 shirt 17 trainers
4 glasses 11 shoes 18 trousers
5 gloves 12 skirt 19 T-shirt
6 handbag 13 socks
7 hat 14 suit

A
B
C
D
E
F
G
H
I
J
K
L
M
N
O
P
Q
R
S

2 Write words 1–10 under the colours.

1 black
2 blue
3 brown
4 green
5 orange
6 pink
7 purple
8 red
9 white
10 yellow

A _____
B _____
C _____
D _____
E _____
F _____
G _____
H _____
I _____
J _____

141

PHOTO BANK

1A Write verbs 1–8 under the photos.

1 be
2 cost
3 listen
4 play
5 read
6 write
7 watch
8 want

A _be_ a teacher

B _____ a newspaper

C _____ to music

D _____ guitar

E _____ ten euros

F _____ TV

G _____ an email

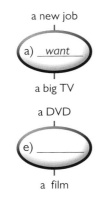
H _____ a car

B Complete the word webs with a verb from 1–8 in Exercise 1A.

a new job
a) _want_
a big TV

twenty-eight
b) _____
hungry

to the teacher
c) _____
to the radio

a book
d) _____
the news online

a DVD
e) _____
a film

tennis
f) _____
golf

a lot
g) _____
five dollars

a blog
h) _____
an email

1 Write the times under the photos.

A _____

B _____

C _____

D _____

E _____

F _____

G _____

H _____

1 Match phrases 1–4 with pictures A–D.

1 get home
2 go to work
3 come home
4 leave home

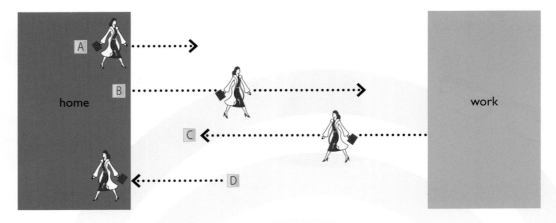

142

DAILY ROUTINES: VERB PHRASES

1A Complete the word webs with a verb in the box.

| ~~have~~ go make get leave start/finish |

a tea
a job — 1 *have* — dinner
a brother

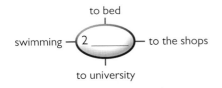

to bed
swimming — 2 _____ — to the shops
to university

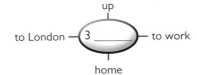

up
to London — 3 _____ — to work
home

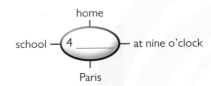

home
school — 4 _____ — at nine o'clock
Paris

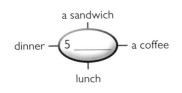

a sandwich
dinner — 5 _____ — a coffee
lunch

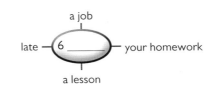

a job
late — 6 _____ — your homework
a lesson

B Work in pairs and take turns. Cover the word webs. Student A: say a verb from the box. Student B: say three verb phrases.

FOOD

1 Match the names of the food with photos A–U.

1 apples
2 bananas
3 beans
4 beef
5 biscuits
6 carrots
7 crisps
8 custard
9 grapes
10 ice cream
11 lamb
12 milk
13 noodles
14 nuts
15 pasta
16 peas
17 potatoes
18 rice
19 sausages
20 tomatoes
21 yoghurt

A
B
C
D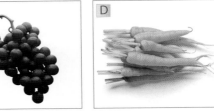
E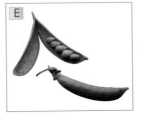
F
G
H
I
J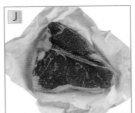
K
L
M
N
O
P
Q
R
S
T
U

PHOTO BANK

1 Match the places with photos A–P.

1 airport
2 bank
3 cinema
4 factory
5 farm
6 gym
7 hospital
8 library
9 museum
10 park
11 post office
12 school
13 shopping centre
14 supermarket
15 theatre
16 zoo

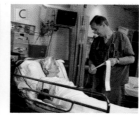

PLACES: SIGNS

1 Match the signs with photos A–J.

1 danger – keep out
2 entrance
3 fire exit
4 look both ways
5 no entry
6 no smoking
7 pull
8 push
9 toilets (Ladies, Gentlemen)
10 way out / exit

DATES: YEARS

1 Match 1–8 with A–H.

1 nineteen eighty-four
2 two thousand and one
3 nineteen ninety-nine
4 sixteen twenty-three
5 two thousand and eight
6 eighteen fifty
7 nineteen forty-five
8 twenty twenty

A **2001**   B **1945**   C **1623**

D **2008**   E **1984**   F **2020**

G **1850**   H **1999**

DATES: TIME PHRASES

1 Match the time phrases with the days/dates/times.

TODAY
FRIDAY
15
JUNE 2012

1 last month
2 last night
3 last week
4 last weekend
5 last year
6 yesterday morning
7 yesterday evening
8 on Tuesday afternoon

a) Saturday June 9 – Sunday June 10
b) Thursday June 14, 6a.m.–12 noon
c) Thursday June 14, 10p.m.– 6a.m.
d) Thursday June 14, 6p.m.–10p.m.
e) May
f) Tuesday June 12, 1p.m.–6p.m.
g) Monday June 4 – Sunday June 9
h) 2011

ADJECTIVES

A

B

C

D

E
Santiago
2500 KM

F

G

H

I

1A Match the adjectives with photos A–I.

1 far *E* _____
2 soft _____
3 heavy _____
4 dark _____
5 long _____
6 full _____
7 expensive _____
8 noisy _____
9 fast _____

B Write the words in the box next to the opposites above.

short   near
light (x2)   quiet
slow   cheap
hard   empty

PHOTO BANK

PREPOSITIONS OF PLACE

 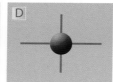
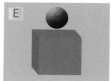 

1A Match the prepositions in the box with pictures A–F.

| in   under   at   on (x 2)   over |

B Correct the sentences about photos 1–6.

1 The cat's over the table.
2 There's a man in a car.
3 There's a plane at the sea.
4 There are two elephants over a river.
5 I live on number sixty-six.
6 Rome is in the River Tiber.

THE WEATHER

1A Match the weather in 1–6 with photos A–F.

1 It was hot and sunny.
2 It was cold. *F*
3 It was cloudy.
4 It was windy.
5 It rained.
6 It snowed.

B Write answers to the questions.

How was the weather:

1 yesterday?
2 last weekend?
3 on your last holiday?
4 on your last birthday?

GIFTS

1A Match the gifts with photos A–O.

1 a bath set
2 a candle
3 a coffee machine
4 a cookbook
5 flowers
6 a gift certificate
7 jewellery
8 perfume
9 a photo frame
10 a plant
11 a scarf
12 a set of glasses
13 a set of luggage
14 socks
15 a vase

B Work in pairs and discuss. Which things are good gifts for you/your best friend/people in your family?

MONEY

1A Match the words with photos A–H.

1 cash
2 a cash machine
3 change
4 a cheque
5 a coin
6 a credit card
7 a note
8 a receipt

B Work in pairs and discuss. Which things do you have in your bag now?

ABILITY VERBS

1 Match the sentences with photos A–J.

1 He can draw.
2 She can't lift it.
3 She can climb.
4 He can throw it.
5 He can't catch.
6 He can't type.
7 She can paint.
8 She can run.
9 She can't hear.
10 She can jump.

1.2

6A Student A: write three *yes/no* questions about photos A–C.

A: Is she an actress? Is she from France? Is she a singer?

Kenji is from Japan. He's an actor.

Fatima is an engineer from Egypt.

It's the city of Oporto, in Portugal.

B Ask Student B your questions about photos A–C.

C Listen to Student B and answer questions about photos D–F.

1.3

1D Student A: read the letters below to Student B.

BBC USA VIP FAQ OK

E Listen to Student B and write the letters.

2.1

6A Student A: look at the photos of your friends. Complete the notes below.

1
Name:
Nationality:
Job:
Where is he now?

2
Names:
Nationalities:
Jobs:
Where are they now?

B Work with other students. Cover your notes and talk about the photos.

2.2

8A Student A: look at the information below. Make questions to find the missing information.

How old is Julia Becker?

Where is she … ?

Gerhardt Becker, 38, and Julia Becker, _____ (age), are husband and wife. Gerhardt is German and Julia is from _____ (country). Their business is in Berlin, and they're _____ (jobs). Their company name is *Rad* and their special taxi-bus is good for families and big groups.

Jon and Liz Henderson are brother and sister, and their Moroccan restaurant, _____ (name), is in Ireland. They're not from Morocco, they're from _____ (country), but their restaurant is very good for Moroccan food.

3.3

7 Student A: you are the waiter. Take the customer's order.

MENU

€1.50   €1.25

€2.00   €1.10

€3.25   €2.95

3.2

8 Student A: ask and answer questions to compare your picture with Student B's. Don't look at Student B's picture. Find six differences between the pictures.

A: In your picture, is Bai's jacket black?
B: No, it isn't. It's …

4.3

5A Student B: look at the information. Write the events and times that Student A suggests.

Saturday	Sunday
10.15a.m. – film	9.30a.m. – festival
2.00p.m. – football match	
	8.15p.m. – concert

A: Let's go to a film on Saturday!
B: What time is it?
A: It's at quarter past ten.
B: OK!

B Ask Student A to come to your events.
B: Let's go to a football match on Saturday.

4.2

6A Student A: work with another Student A and look at Yong's desk. Say five things about Yong.

He studies English.

COMMUNICATION BANK

5.3

6B Student B: you are a hotel receptionist. Read the information and answer Student A's questions.

Hotel money exchange at reception:
8.30a.m.–12.30p.m. and 4.30p.m.–6.30p.m.

Lunch: hotel café: 12p.m.–3p.m.

Guided walking tour of the town: 9.30a.m., 12.30p.m., 3.30p.m. €25.

Café Slavia: 8a.m.–11p.m.

Opera at the National Theatre: 8p.m., €35

6.2

5A Student A: answer Student B's questions about Venice and London.

A: Is there a train from the airport to Venice?
B: No, there isn't.

	Venice	London (Heathrow)
train / from the airport?	no	£18
underground?	no	£5
airport bus?	€3	£15
other information?	waterbus, €20	train tickets £16.50 online, £23 on the train

B Ask Student B questions to complete the information for Barcelona and Edinburgh.

B: Is there a train from the airport to Barcelona?
A: Yes, there is. It's three euros.

	Barcelona	Edinburgh
train / from the airport?		
underground?		
airport bus?		
other information?		

C What's the best way to go from the airport to the centre in these four cities?

6.3

6A Student B: you work in a ticket office in the bus station in Amsterdam. Look at the information and answer Student A's questions.

ticket	a single to Brussels
price	€14
time of next bus	9a.m.
gate	4
arrival time	2.15p.m.

B Change roles. Student B: you are at the central train station in Amsterdam. You want to buy a ticket. Ask Student A questions to complete the table.

ticket	a return to Paris
price	
time of next train	
platform	
arrival time	

REVIEW 4: UNITS 7–8

4A Students A and B: work in pairs. Read the situation and answer the questions.

On Monday at half past one in the afternoon there was a robbery at a clothes shop. You were the robbers! You said you were at a restaurant, but you weren't.

1 Where was the robbery?
2 Where were the robbers?
3 Were you at the restaurant?

B Work in pairs and write answers to the police's questions. Do not tell the truth!

1 What time did you arrive at the restaurant?
2 What was the name of the restaurant?
3 What type of restaurant was it?
4 What did you eat?
5 How much did it cost?

C Write down other important information.

D Work in groups and answer the police's questions.

9.3

5C Student A: ask Student B the questions.

1 Where were you this time last year?
2 What was your first teacher's name?
3 Spell your first name backwards (e.g. John: n-h-o-J).
4 What would you like for your next meal?

6.1

6 Student A: ask and answer questions to compare your picture with Student B's. Don't look at Student B's picture. Find five differences between the two pictures.

A: Are there two hotels in your picture?
B: No, there's one hotel. That's one difference!

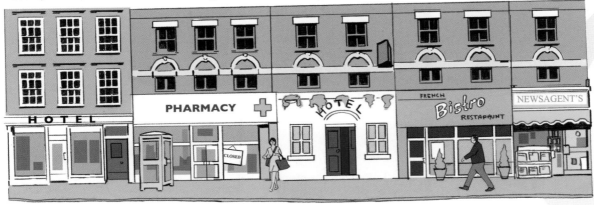

3.2

8 Student B: ask and answer questions to compare your picture with Student A's. Don't look at Student A's picture. Find six differences between your pictures.

B: In your picture, are Paul's trousers black?
A: No, they aren't. They're …

7.4

3D Work in groups. Do the quiz. Use the key phrases from page 81 to help.

* Nelson Mandela was free
* Obama was the new president of the USA
* The end of the Berlin Wall
* YouTube started
* Russian Yuri Gagarin was the first man in space
* September 11 terrorist attacks in the USA
* Princess Diana died

1961 1989 1990 1997 2001 2005 2008

E Turn to page 153 to check your answers.

1.2

6A Student B: write three *yes/no* questions about photos D–F.

B: *Is he a doctor? Is he from China? Is he a businessman?*

Yolanda is from England. She's a sports teacher.

Niko is a taxi driver from Greece.

It's the city of Kobe, in Japan.

B Listen to Student A and answer questions about photos A–C.

C Ask Student A your questions about photos D–F.

1.3

1D Student B: listen to Student A and write the letters.

E Read the letters below to Student A.

DVD   EU   WWW   IBM   UK

2.1

6A Student B: look at the photos of your friends. Complete the notes below.

1
Name:
Nationality:
Job:
Where is she now?

2
Names:
Nationalities:
Jobs:
Where are they now?

B Work with other students. Cover your notes and talk about the photos.

3.3

7 Student B: you are the customer. You have nine euros. Order food and drink for two people.

9.3

5C Student B: ask Student A the questions.

1 What's your favourite colour?
2 Count backwards from 10–1.
3 Where were you this time last week?
4 Would you like a cat?

10.1

6B

Section A: 10+ points. You're good at the arts, so maybe the best job for you is a singer, an actor, a dancer or a musician. But maybe you don't like singing and dancing in front of a lot of people. That's OK, you can teach other people.

Section B: 10+ points. OK, you're active and sporty, but there aren't a lot of jobs for sportsmen or women. You can play sports at the weekend and get a job in the week teaching sports in a school or a gym. Or maybe you can be a salesperson in a sports shop.

Section C: 10+ points. You're good with your head. Maybe an office job is best for you, but do you like working with people? Then how about a job in a bank or as a manager in a big company? Do you like working alone? Then maybe a job with computers is good for you.

10+ points in no sections? Don't worry, there's a job for you … but we can't tell you what it is! What do you think?

6.1

6 Student B: ask and answer questions to compare your picture with Student A's. Don't look at Student A's picture. Find five differences between the two pictures.

A: Are there two hotels in your picture?
B: No, there's one hotel. That's one difference!

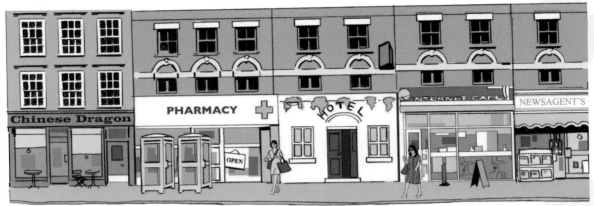

REVIEW 1: UNITS 1–2

5 Student A: look at the table and ask questions to complete the information.

First name	¹Frank	²Fatimah	³Neil and Sandra
Family name	Cho		Macdonald
Nationality		English	
Age	28		23 and 20
Job		nurse	
Email address		faha@ yahoo.com	

B: Number one is Frank. What's his family name?
A: Cho.
B: How do you spell it?
A: C-h-o. What's his nationality?

5.3

6C Student A: you are a hotel receptionist. Read the information and answer Student B's questions.

Hotel money exchange at reception:
9.30a.m.–12.30p.m. and 3.30p.m.–8.30p.m.

Lunch: hotel café: 11.30a.m.–3.30p.m.

Guided walking tour of the town: 10a.m., 1.15p.m., 6.30p.m., €20 (evening €30)

Café Milena: 10a.m.–8p.m.

Opera at the Prague State Opera: 7p.m., €50

4.2

6A Student B: work with another Student B and look at Danny's desk. Say five things about Danny.

He studies Portuguese.

7.4

Key to quiz

1961	Russian Yuri Gagarin was the first man in space
1989	The end of the Berlin Wall
1990	Nelson Mandela was free
1997	Princess Diana died
2001	September 11 terrorist attacks in the USA
2005	YouTube started
2008	Obama was the new president of the USA

AUDIO SCRIPTS

LEAD-IN Recording 4

Conversation 1
A: OK, Antonio. What's 'libro' in English?
B: Sorry, I don't know.
A: It's 'book'.
B: Can you write it, please?
A: Yes …

Conversation 2
A: OK. Open your books, please.
B: Sorry, I don't understand.
A: Open, like this.
B: Which page?
A: Page eight.
B: Can you repeat that, please?
A: Yes, page eight.
B: Thank you.

UNIT 1 Recording 1

Conversation 1
A: Hello, I'm Simon.
B: Hi, I'm Carmen.
A: Nice to meet you.
B: Nice to meet you, too.
A: Where are you from?
B: I'm from Spain.
A: Oh, where in Spain?
B: From Madrid.

Conversation 2
A: Hello, I'm Dave.
B: Hi, I'm Cindy.
A: Nice to meet you.
B: Nice to meet you, too.
A: Where are you from?
B: I'm from the US.
A: Oh, where in the US?
B: From New York.

Conversation 3
A: Hi, I'm Sue.
B: Hello, I'm Tom.
A: Nice to meet you.
B: Nice to meet you, too.
A: Where are you from?
B: I'm from Australia
A: Oh. Are you from Sydney?
B: No, I'm not. I'm from Melbourne.

Conversation 4
A: Hi, I'm Martin.
B: Hi, I'm Katie.
A: Nice to meet you.
B: Nice to meet you, too.
A: Are you from Ireland?
B: Yes, I am.
A: Oh, where in Ireland?
B: From Dublin.

UNIT 1 Recording 3

Conversation 1
A: Hello, I'm Janet.
B: Hi, I'm Paul. Nice to meet you.
A: Nice to meet you, too. Where are you from?
B: I'm from South Africa.
A: Oh, where in South Africa?
B: From Cape Town.

Conversation 2
A: Hello, I'm Kasia.

B: Hi, I'm Peter.
A: Nice to meet you.
B: Nice to meet you, too. Where are you from?
A: I'm from Poland.
B: Are you from Warsaw?
A: No, I'm not. I'm from Gdansk.

UNIT 1 Recording 6

1 He's an actor.
2 She's a student.
3 Is he from India?
4 Is it your first time here?
5 Yes, it is.

UNIT 1 Recording 9

Conversation 1
A: Good evening. Can I help you?
B: My name's Taylor. Frances Taylor.
A: How do you spell that?
B: T-a-y-l-o-r.
A: T-a-y-l-o-r.
B: Yes.
A: And your first name?
B: It's Frances.
A: F-r-a-n-c … is it i-s?
B: No, e. E as in England. F-r-a-n-c-e-s.
A: Thanks. OK, here's your visitor's card. You're in studio 379.
B: Thank you.
A: You're welcome.

Conversation 2
A: Can I help you?
B: Yes, I'm a student, a new student.
A: Welcome to the school. What's your family name?
B: Almeida.
A: How do you spell Almeida?
B: A-l-m-e-i-d-a.
A: And what's your first name?
B: Anabella.
A: OK, Anabella. Here's your student card.
B: Thank you. Oh, my first name's wrong.
A: Oh, sorry. How do you spell it?
B: It's Anabella, A-n-a-b-e-l-l-a.
A: A-n-a-b-e-l-l-a.
B: That's right.
A: OK, Anabella. You're in room 124.
B: 124?
A: Yes.

Conversation 3
A: OK, what's your family name?
B: Young, Y-o-u-n-g.
A: Ah-huh. And what's your first name?
B: Stefanie.
A: How do you spell that?
B: S-t-e-f-a-n-i-e.
A: Ah yes, for the fitness class in room ten.
B: That's right.
A: What's your phone number?
B: Er … it's oh five three two, four one nine.
A: And what's your email address?
B: It's stef at yahoo dot com.
A: OK, thank you.

UNIT 1 Recording 12

Hello, or 'dia duit' from Ireland. My name's
Kaitlin and I'm from Dublin, the capital city of

Ireland. Dublin's a beautiful city. It isn't very
big but it's very old. I'm a tourist information
assistant, at the tourist information office in
the centre of Dublin. So of course, English is
important for my job. The countryside in Ireland
is beautiful with mountains, rivers and the sea.
The villages are old and beautiful. Goodbye, or
'slan' in Irish.

UNIT 2 Recording 2

Conversation 1
B: Hi, Erika. Coffee?
A: No thanks.
B: Hey, photos. Let's see …
A: Yes, from the party.
B: The party?
A: Yes, my daughter's birthday. At the weekend.
B: Oh, great. Is this your family?
A: Yes, me, my husband, my two sons and my daughter.
B: And where are you?
A: We're at home in …

Conversation 2
B: Oh, and is this your mother?
A: Yes, this is my mum. And me, of course.
B: And the birthday cake.
A: Yes.
B: What's your mother's name?
A: Margit.
B: Margaret?
A: Well, yes, Margaret in English. Margit in Hungarian.
B: Are you Hungarian? You and your mother?
A: Yes.
B: You aren't English?
A: No, we aren't English!
B: Really, your English is very good!
A: Well thanks but …

Conversation 3
A: This is me and Tim.
B: Your husband.
A: Yeah.
B: Is he Hungarian too?
A: No, he's English.
B: I see. And what's his job?
A: He's a businessman.
B: A businessman. What business is he in?
A: The hotel and restaurant business.
B: Hmm …

Conversation 4
A: … and this is a photo of the children.
B: Oh, it's a great picture.
A: Yeah.
B: And this is the birthday girl?
A: Yes, our daughter Florence. We call her Flori.
B: Ahhh. How old is she?
A: She's seven now.
B: And your sons …
A: Yes, Johnny and Lewis.
B: Are they students?
A: Yes. Johnny's at the University of London.
B: And Lewis?
A: Lewis is at music school. He's a musician. Guitar, piano …
B: Really? That's great …

UNIT 2 Recording 4

1 We're from England.
2 They're actors.
3 We're in Japan.
4 You're right.
5 We're in class.
6 They're here.

UNIT 2 Recording 8

Conversation 1
A: Good class.
B: Yes.
A: I'm hungry.
B: Yeah, me too. Let's eat.
A: OK, where?
B: Erm … that Italian café? What's its name?
A: Lugo?
B: Yeah, let's go to Café Lugo.
A: OK. Good idea.

Conversation 2
A: Hello, are you Mr Tajima?
B: Yes.
A: I'm Lee Smith.
B: Oh, hello. Nice to meet you, Mr Smith.
A: Nice to meet you, too.
B: Erm … let's sit down. Coffee?
A: Yes, please.

Conversation 3
A: Let's have a break.
B: Good idea. I'm tired
A: Me too.
B: … and hot.
A: Yeah. Let's stop.
B: Yeah, OK. Let's have a cola.
A: OK.

UNIT 2 Recording 9

1 Let's eat.
2 Let's sit down.
3 Let's have a break.
4 Let's stop.
5 Let's have a cola.

UNIT 2 Recording 10

1 A: Let's have a break.
B: Good idea.
2 A: Let's sit down.
B: OK.
3 A: Let's have a coffee.
B: OK.
4 A: Let's walk.
B: OK.

UNIT 2 Recording 11

OK, five people in my life. The first is Duncan. Duncan's my brother. He's thirty-one and he's a businessman. And Sarah … Sarah's a very good friend, my best friend really. She's from Scotland and she's a teacher. We are on the phone a lot! She's great. And this, this is Mark. I'm an office worker and Mark's my manager but he's very nice, very friendly. And Wendy is in my class. We're in a Spanish class together. Our teacher is Rosa. She's from Madrid in Spain and Wendy and I sit together in the class and now we're friends. The class is good … but our Spanish isn't very good!

REVIEW 1 Recording 1

Conversation 1
A: Hello, I'm Tony Morelli.
B: Hi, I'm Frank Cho.
A: Nice to meet you.
B: Nice to meet you, too. Is Morelli an Italian name?
A: Yes, it is, but I'm American.
B: I see.
A: And are you from China?
B: No, Cho is a Korean name. I'm from Korea. It's good music, yeah?
A: Yeah, it's good. The singer is my friend …

Conversation 2
A: Hi, I'm Fatimah.
B: Hello, my name's Terry. Terry Gonzales.
A: Nice to meet you.
B: And you. Is Fatimah your family name or your first name?
A: It's my first name. It's an Arabic name.
B: Where are you from?
A: My father's from Egypt, but I'm English. And you? Is Gonzales a Spanish name?
B: Yes, it is but I'm not from Spain, I'm from Colombia.
A: Oh, where in Colombia?
B: Bogotá.
A: Hey, I'm hungry.
B: Me too. Let's go and eat something.
A: Good idea. So, what … ?

Conversation 3
A: Brad Churchill, nice to meet you.
B: Sue Takahashi. Nice to meet you, too.
A: Your English is very good!
B: Thanks, but I'm from Canada.
A: Oh, I'm sorry. But Takahashi is a Japanese name.
B: Yes, my family is from Japan, but I'm Canadian.
A: Ah. Yes, my name's Churchill, very English! But I'm Australian, from Sydney.
B: Oh, I know Sydney.
A: Really? Hey, let's go and have a coffee.
B: OK, yeah I …

UNIT 3 Recording 2

Conversation 1
A: Congratulations, Sam, and welcome to the company.
B: Thank you, Mr Stanford.
A: Bill.
B: Thank you … Bill.
A: These are your keys.
B: My keys?
A: Yes, keys to the building and the office. And the company car.
B: Great, thanks.

Conversation 2
A: Hey, Anne. What's that?
B: This is my new phone, my work phone.
A: Nice.
C: Ahem.
B: Yeah, some great games. Look at this, Jill.
A: Oooh …
B: And music.
A: Wow, great.

C: AHEM!
B: And here's a video of my baby.
C: Sorry, ladies. Lovely phone, but is this a coffee break?
A: Oh, sorry Mr Fletcher. Hmm … Good idea. Let's have a break!

Conversation 3
A: Thanks, Janet.
B: No problem. What's in this box? It's very heavy.
A: It's my new printer.
B: And what's in those boxes?
A: Oh, these small boxes are my office things. Oh, be careful!
B: Oh, no. Denise, I'm so sorry.
A: Oh, no. My new printer.
B: I'm so sorry …

Conversation 4
A: … and come in here. This is my home office.
B: OK. And is that your new computer?
A: Yeah, it is.
B: Nice. Is it good?
A: Yeah.
B: Expensive?
A: Erm … yeah.

UNIT 3 Recording 5

A These are Elvis Presley's white trousers from a concert in Nashville.
B I'm sure you know this from photos of Marilyn Monroe. It's her black jacket.
C This is very famous. It's Michael Jackson's red shirt from the 1990s.
D This is from a tennis match in Mexico in 2009. It's Venus Williams's blue hat. It's the winner's hat.
E This is a typical schoolboy sweater, so you probably know it's Harry Potter's brown sweater.
F That's Usain Bolt's yellow t-shirt. It's his t-shirt for running.

UNIT 3 Recording 6

Conversation 1
A: Can I have a coffee, please?
B: With milk?
A: No thanks. Black.
B: Sugar?
A: Yes, please. One.
B: One black coffee with sugar! That's five euros.

Conversation 2
A: Can I have two coffees, please?
B: Espresso or cappuccino?
A: Oh, espresso, please.
B: Anything else?
A: No thanks. How much is that?
B: That's four euros fifty.

Conversation 3
A: Hi.
B: Hi. Can I have an egg sandwich, please?
A: White or brown bread?
B: Oh, brown bread, please.
A: Anything else?
B: Yeah, can I have one of those cakes?
A: These ones?
B: No, the chocolate ones.
A: Anything to drink?

155

AUDIO SCRIPTS

B: Yes, a mineral water, please. How much is that?
A: That's two euros for the sandwich, one for the cake and one for the mineral water. That's four euros.
B: Here you are.

Conversation 4

A: Can I have a mineral water, please?
B: Still or sparkling?
A: Sparkling, please.
B: Anything else?
A: No, thank you. How much is that?
B: That's two euros.

UNIT 3   Recording 10

A: Excuse me.
B: Yes.
A: Where are those lamps from?
B: They're from Turkey.
A: Can I have a look?
B: Yes. This one?
A: No, that one. The blue one.
B: It's very nice.
A: How much is it?
B: It's two hundred.
A: That's expensive. Hmm. Fifty.
B: One hundred and fifty.
A: Seventy-five.
B: For you, a special discount. Only one hundred.
A: OK. One hundred.
B: It's a very good price.

UNIT 4   Recording 1

A: Excuse me. Do you have a moment?
B: Yes?
A: You aren't American?
B: No, no, I'm from Japan. I'm on holiday here.
A: OK. So, my question is: what's different for you about life here?
B: Erm … well, here people live in houses … they live in big houses. I'm from Tokyo, and we live in flats, small flats. So that's very different.
A: … and so for you, what's different about life here?
C: Erm … well I study at university here. And it's very different from my country because here in the United States, the students have jobs. They work in the evenings, maybe ten hours a week.
A: And you? Do you work?
C: Me? No, I don't. I don't have time. And in my country students don't work, they only study.
D: What's different here? Erm … oh yeah, people drive everywhere. I mean, they drive two hundred metres to the shops.
A: Do you have a car?
D: Yes, I do, but I don't drive to the shops. Not two hundred metres! I walk.
A: And where are you from?
D: I'm from England.
E: I think it's not so different. I'm from Italy and my American friends are not so different from me. Er … we like sport … we like clothes … We, er … we go to the cinema, restaurants, have a coffee …
A: So you like the same things.
E: Yeah, the same … not different.

UNIT 4   Recording 5

Conversation 1

A: Excuse me, what time is it?
B: It's four o'clock.
A: Thank you. Oh, and do you know … where's the music festival?
B: You go down here and …

Conversation 2

A: Hi, Lisa.
B: Hi, Manuel. Come and sit down.
A: It's time for class.
B: What time's the lesson?
A: At half past three. New time.
B: Oh, no. We're late.
A: Yeah, let's go.

Conversation 3

A: Excuse me. What time is the film?
B: At quarter to nine and half past ten.
A: Oh, that's late. Is there an early one?
B: Hmmm … yeah, at quarter past six.

Conversation 4

A: The World Cup Final is on TV tomorrow!
B: What time's the match?
A: Erm … at quarter past two.
B: Quarter past two. Thanks.

Conversation 5

A: We're late again.
B: No, we're not. It's a party. It's OK to be late.
A: What time is it now?
B: It's quarter to eleven.
A: Quarter to eleven?
B: It's OK …

Conversation 6

A: What time is the concert?
B: At quarter past seven.
A: Sorry? When?
B: Quarter past seven.
A: Quarter past seven. Thanks.

UNIT 4   Recording 7

A: Sorry? When?

UNIT 4   Recording 8

My favourite season is autumn. I like it because it's not too hot and not too cold. I don't like the summer or the winter because I don't like very hot or very cold weather. In autumn, the trees are beautiful … all red and yellow. At the weekend, I walk with my family in the mountains. My favourite holiday is in autumn. It's Thanksgiving, and it's in November. The family comes together for a big dinner. I also like autumn because it's the start of the school year. I know some people don't like school, but I'm a teacher and I like it!

REVIEW 2   Recording 1

A: So if I press this …
B: Beth, who's that?
A: These are my favourite people.
B: That woman. She's beautiful.
A: William! That's my sister Alicia. Watch it!
B: Your sister? Oh … who's that then?
A: That's Keith. He's a good friend from university.
B: Do you meet a lot now?

A: No, but we email each other every day.
B: And this?
A: Monique, from work.
B: Are you friends?
A: Not really. But I like her a lot.
B: And if I press this … Oh, look!
A: Yeah, Paris …
B: … Cairo … and the Great Wall of China. Big traveller!
A: Yeah, then here …
B: Hey, nice dress.
A: You know that dress. My black party dress.
B: Yeah, I like that dress. Oh, you like the BBC.
A: Yeah, the website's great for the news.
B: Let's look at … What's this? Ice cream?
A: Yeah, from the Gelatino Café. I love it. But I don't go there a lot.
B: And what's this?
A: Johnny Depp.
B: Is he one of your favourite people?
A: No, but *Pirates of the Caribbean* is one of my favourite films.
B: And here's another film. *Pirates of the Caribbean II*. Johnny Depp again and here's …
A: OK, that's enough …

UNIT 5   Recording 2

Conversation 1

A: How's the family?
B: Fine. Well, you remember Clara?
A: Clara, your daughter? Yes, how old is she now?
B: She's seventeen.
A: She isn't at school?
B: No.
A: Does she have a job?
B: No, she doesn't. That's the problem.
A: So what does she do all day?
B: Well, she listens to her music and … and she sleeps a lot.
A: What time does she get up?
B: I don't know because I'm at work. At the weekend she gets up at eleven.
A: Does she want a job?
B: I don't know. She doesn't talk much.
A: What do you mean?
B: Well, for example, in the evenings, we have dinner together. But Clara just sits there and listens to her music. Or she answers her phone and talks to her friends, but not to her family. It drives me crazy.
A: Does she … ?

Conversation 2

A: Hi, Paula.
B: Hi. What's the problem? You look bad.
A: It's Julio.
B: Julio?
A: Yeah. Well, he doesn't listen to me.
B: What do you mean?
A: Well, I talk about my problems and he just checks his text messages or watches TV.
B: Does he talk to you?
A: Yeah … well, no … he says 'Mmmm'.
B: 'Mmmm'! What does that mean?
A: It means he doesn't really listen.
B: Oh, my boyfriend is exactly the same.

Conversation 3

A: Hey, Wayne. What's up? You look tired.

B: Yeah. No sleep.
A: What's the problem?
B: Neighbours. Problem neighbours. Or just one, the man in the flat upstairs.
A: Why? Does he play loud music? Big parties?
B: No, he doesn't. The problem is he works at night. He goes to work at six in the evening. I get home and I see him go to work every night.
A: What's his job?
B: He sells coffee in a snack bar at the train station.
A: And when does he get home?
B: About half past four. And then he watches television for two or three hours.
A: So when does he go to bed?
B: Oh, about six or seven.
A: And what time do you get up?
B: Huh! Now I get up at five. It's impossible to sleep. So I listen to music, drink coffee then I go to work around eight.
A: And when do you go to bed?
B: Late. Midnight or 1am.
A: Ooh, four hours' sleep. Not good.

UNIT 5 Recording 6

A: Excuse me?
B: Yes, can I help you?
A: I have a reservation for tonight.
B: And your name?
A: Shannon.
B: Ah, yes. Miss Shannon. A single for two nights.
A: That's right.
B: I'm sorry, but your room isn't ready yet.
A: Oh, am I early? What time is check-in?
B: 2p.m. usually. Your room is almost ready. Please have a seat.
A: Thank you. I have one question.
B: Yes?
A: When does the gym open?
B: It opens from 6a.m. to 10p.m., except lunchtime. It closes from twelve to one.
A: Lovely. Oh, just one more question. What time is breakfast?
B: From half past six to nine o'clock.
A: And where is it?
B: In the restaurant, over there.
A: Thank you.

A: Excuse me?
B: Yes?
A: Me again. I have one more question.
B: Sure.
A: Do you have a hairdresser's in the hotel?
B: Yes, it opens every day except Monday.
A: And today's Monday.
B: Yes, I'm sorry. But it opens tomorrow.
A: That's good.
B: From ten to six. Actually, I'm wrong. On Tuesdays, it closes at nine o'clock in the evening.
A: That's great, thank you.

B: Excuse me, madam.
A: Yes?
B: Your room's ready now. Here's your key card. Room 538 on the fifth floor.
A: Wonderful, thank you.
B: You're welcome. Enjoy your stay.
A: Oh, but I have one more question.
B: Yes?
A: I want to go on a guided tour of the old

town. Do you know a good one?
B: Ah, yes. We do a tour from the hotel.
A: Oh good. When does the tour leave?
B: It leaves at 9a.m. and at 3p.m.
A: How much does it cost?
B: It costs fifteen euros.
A: Great. Thank you.
B: Any more questions I can help you with?
A: No, thank you. Oh, just one …

UNIT 5 Recording 8

A: When does the gym open?
B: It opens from 6a.m. to 10p.m., except lunchtime. It closes from twelve to one.
A: Lovely. Oh, just one …

A: Do you have a hairdresser's in the hotel?
B: Yes, it opens every day except Monday.
A: And today's Monday.
B: Yes, I'm sorry. But it opens tomorrow.
A: That's good.
B: From ten to six. Actually, I'm wrong. On Tuesdays it closes at nine o'clock in the evening.
A: That's great, thank you.

B: Your room's ready now. Here's your key card. Room 538 on the fifth floor.
A: Wonderful, thank you.
B: You're welcome.

A: I want to go on a guided tour of the old town. Do you know a good one?
B: Ah, yes. We do a tour from the hotel.
A: Oh good. When does the tour leave?
B: It leaves at 9a.m. and at 3p.m.
A: And how much does it cost?
B: It costs fifteen euros.
A: Great. Thank you.

UNIT 5 Recording 10

A: What's on your list?
B: Well, number one on my list is fruit.
A: Fruit? Why fruit?
B: It's good for you.
A: Do you really like it?
B: I like bananas and apples.
A: Bananas and apples. That's two things.
B: OK, fine. One is bananas and two is apples.
A: And what's number three on your list?
B: Number three is ice cream. I love ice cream.
A: Me too. It's on my list.
B: Maybe it's bad for you, but …
A: Ice cream and fruit. That's OK.
B: Yeah, with fruit, it's good.
A: And number four?
B: Pasta with cheese.
A: Mmm … that's two …
B: No, I think it's one. I eat pasta every day. With butter, with cheese …
A: Yeah.
B: And number five is cereal.
A: Really? Do you really like cereal?
B: I do, yes.
A: What about drinks?
B: Milk for my cereal.
A: Yes. And what other drink do you have?
B: I have tea. English tea.
A: Of course. Me too.

UNIT 6 Recording 2

A: Excuse me … ?
B: Sorry, I'm in a hurry.
A: Excuse me?
C: Yes?
A: Is there a train to Paris tonight?
C: No, sorry, there aren't any trains tonight. It's the weather. It's very bad.
A: Not any trains? Not one?
C: No, not tonight. Maybe tomorrow. They …
D: Hello? Pete, where are you?
A: Hi, I'm here in London, in the station, but there aren't any trains and … Oh, no … Excuse me, is there a payphone near here? My phone's dead.
E: Yes, there's a payphone over there.
A: Thanks. Oh, and is there an internet café?
E: Erm … I don't think so. No, there isn't an internet café. Not in the station but there's one in Judd Street.
A: Judd Street. Thanks.
F: Can I help you?
A: Yes. Are there any restaurants in the station?
F: Yes, there are … but … what's the time?
A: Half past eleven.
F: Ah, they're closed now, but there's a snack bar over there. That's open.
A: And is there a cash machine here?
F: Yes, over there.
A: Thanks. And hotels?
F: There are two hotels near here. The Charlotte Street Hotel … that's about two hundred and fifty pounds a night.
A: Two hundred and fifty pounds? That's expensive.
F: And there's the Ridgemount, that's about eighty pounds.
A: Where's that?
F: It's here on the map.
A: OK … thank you for your help.

UNIT 6 Recording 5

A: A ticket to Amsterdam, please.
B: Single or return?
A: Return, please.
B: Leaving today?
A: Yes.
B: When do you want to come back?
A: Tomorrow afternoon.
B: OK. That's twenty-nine euros.
A: What time's the next bus?
B: There's one at half past two.
A: What time does it arrive in Amsterdam?
B: At quarter past four. Here's your ticket.
A: Thanks a lot.
B: The bus leaves from gate twenty-four.
A: Sorry? Gate thirty-four?
B: No, gate twenty-four.
A: Thanks a lot.

UNIT 6 Recording 6

A: A ticket to Amsterdam, please.
B: Single or return?
A: Return, please.
B: Leaving today?
A: Yes.
B: When do you want to come back?
A: Tomorrow afternoon.

B: OK. That's twenty-nine euros.
A: What time's the next bus?
B: There's one at half past two.
A: What time does it arrive in Amsterdam?
B: At quarter past four. Here's your ticket.
A: Thanks a lot.
B: The bus leaves from gate twenty-four.

UNIT 6 Recording 8

I live in London but I'm from the countryside.
British people love their cars, but it's expensive
to drive in London. There's a good public
transport system and a lot of people use the
underground or buses. Some people go to
work by bike but I don't. I think bikes are
dangerous in the city. The best way to travel is
by underground, but it's very crowded in the
mornings. In the countryside, a lot of people
drive, of course, or they use buses. In my village,
I go everywhere by bike.

REVIEW 3 Recording 1

Conversation 1
A: Excuse me.
B: Yeah.
A: There's a problem with my coffee. It's cold.
B: Oh, sorry. Let me get you another one.
A: Thanks.

Conversation 2
A: Do you have The New York Times?
B: Sorry, we don't. We usually have it, but not
today.
A: Oh. Well, do you have any other newspapers
in English?
B: We have The Times.
A: That's a British paper, yeah?
B: That's right.
A: Hmm, no thanks. I really want an American
paper.

Conversation 3
A: OK, let's get some money out.
B: What's the problem?
A: It says there isn't any money in the machine.
B: Oh, no.
A: Maybe it's because it's a bank holiday. Look, I
have some money. Let's go to Salvatore's café. It
isn't expensive.

Conversation 4
A: Excuse me.
B: Is there a problem?
A: Yes, I'm in number three and the computer's
broken.
B: Let me see. Ah, yes, there's a problem. Please
try number five.

Conversation 5
A: Can I help you?
B: Yes, I'm not very well. I'm very hot and I'm
tired all the time. Do you have something to
help?
A: These are good. Go home and go to bed.
B: How much are they?
A: Five euros.
B: Five euros. Hmm, no thank you.

UNIT 7 Recording 1

1 I was at home with my parents and my
brother and sister. There was a family party,
but nothing really special. There were fireworks

on TV … but I think I was asleep at midnight. I
don't really remember.
2 We were in Miami, Florida, at a concert. The
bands were great – the Gipsy Kings and some
other local bands. It was great.
3 I was at work in London. I work at a club,
and of course it was a very big night for us. The
money was good. Everybody was happy, crazy.
There were fantastic fireworks over the River
Thames.
4 I was on a beach in Fiji with my friends. There
was a beautiful sunrise. We were the first
people to see the start of the year 2000. And
we weren't alone – there were hundreds of
people on the beach with us. It was a beautiful
morning, very peaceful …
5 I was in hospital. I was born on January 1st,
2000. My mother says there was a party.
Maybe it was for the New Year … or was the
party for me?

UNIT 7 Recording 9

Conversation 1
A: Hey, let's go!
B: What?
A: Let's go!
B: Why?
A: The film. It's terrible.
B: Really? I think it's great!
A: Oh, come on. Let's just go.
B: No, let's stay. Here, have a sweet.
A: Thanks a lot.

Conversation 2
A: How was your steak?
B: Delicious, just right. I really liked it. How was
your chicken?
A: Urgh, I didn't like it. It wasn't very good.
B: Oh, well here's the ice cream. Thank you.
Mmm, this is good.
A: Yes, this is nice.

Conversation 3
A: Hi.
B: Hi. How was the concert?
A: Fantastic! I loved it! The band was fantastic
and the singer … she was great!
B: Oh, yeah, she is good.
A: So, are you free tomorrow?

Conversation 4
A: Hi, Mary. How are you?
B: Fine, thanks and you?
A: I'm OK. Um, were you at Warren's party last
night?
B: Yeah.
A: How was it?
B: It was all right …
A: But … ?
B: Mmm. Well, it was boring – there weren't a
lot of people there.
A: Ah.
B: So where were you?
A: Ah, well. I was at Alan's party.
B: Alan's party?
A: Yeah, uh, sorry …
B: Oh. How was it?
A: Er … it was very good.

UNIT 7 Recording 11

A: OK, so which was first?
B: I think Chernobyl was first.
A: Yes, I agree. But which date – 1986 or 1991?
B: I think it was 1986.
A: OK let's put that. So, what was next?
B: I think Google started.
A: I'm not sure. Maybe the Asian tsunami?
B: No, Google was before the Asian tsunami.
A: OK. Which date?
B: Erm … 1991, I think.
A: OK. 1991.
B: And I think the Asian tsunami was next, in
2004. I remember it well. It was in December at
the end of the year.
A: OK, so that's 2004. And Michael Jackson?
B: He died in 2009, I think.
A: 2009. Right, let's check the answers.
A: OK, we were right about three answers. The
Chernobyl nuclear accident was in 1986, the
Asian tsunami was in 2004 and Michael Jackson
died in 2009.
B: But we were wrong about Google?
A: Yes. Google didn't start in 1991. It started in
1996.

UNIT 8 Recording 2

A: Welcome to Good and Bad. This week we
talk about holidays – good ones and bad ones.
Our hotline is 123 2222. And here's our first
caller. Hello, Ken?
B: Hi.
A: So, tell us about your two holidays.
B: Yeah, well my family went camping in Canada
when I was twelve. We had one tent for six
people, and we didn't have water or electricity.
A: Oh, right. Did you like it?
B: Yes, I did. It was … fantastic. No TV, no
internet … we cooked on a fire and played
games.
A: Sounds great. And your other holiday?
B: Last year I went to Sydney with my girlfriend. I
lost my passport on the first day.
A: Sorry to hear that.
B: But Sydney was beautiful. We saw some
interesting buildings and lovely museums … but
then I ate some bad food … fish … and I was
very ill.
A: Ow. So that was a bad holiday. But as you say
Sydney's a beautiful city.
B: Yes, it is.
A: OK, Ken. Thank you for calling. Next caller,
Clare? Are you there?
C: Yeah, hello.
A: Hi. Tell us about your holidays.
B: Well, last year we went to France.
A: Oh, where did you go?
B: We went to Paris, but … there was a
problem with the plane. We waited for ten
hours at the airport. Then they said there
weren't any seats on the next plane. Or the
next plane.
A: Oh, no! What did you do?
B: We went by train! We had five hours in Paris
then we came home.
A: By plane?
B: No, by train. We had dinner on the train.
Expensive sandwiches.
A: So that wasn't very good. How about your

other holiday? The good one?

C: Ah yes, it was in China. I was there for two months. I was alone, so I met a lot of local people. They were very nice.

A: Did you speak English with them?

C: No, I didn't. I spoke a little Chinese and they liked that.

A: Great. Thanks, Clare. And next we have Dan. Hi, Dan.

D: Hi.

A: Is your first holiday good or bad?

D: Good – really good. I went to Peru. It was a walking holiday and it was wonderful.

A: Why was that?

D: Well, I went with a friend and we …

UNIT 8 Recording 4

Conversation 1

A: Excuse me, where's the fruit?

B: Do you see the vegetables over there?

A: Vegetables? What are they?

B: Vegetables … you know, tomatoes, potatoes, carrots.

A: Oh, vegetables.

B: Yeah. Vegetables.

A: OK … vegetables.

B: The fruit's behind the vegetables.

A: Sorry?

B: You see the vegetables? They're in front of the fruit. Over there.

A: Let me check. The fruit's behind the vegetables.

B: Yes, that's right.

A: Oh, OK. Thanks.

B: No problem.

Conversation 2

A: Excuse me, where's the bread?

B: Er … Do you see the snacks?

A: Snacks? I don't know 'snacks'.

B: Snacks, for example, chocolate, nuts and crisps.

A: Oh, I understand.

B: The bread is on the right of the snacks.

A: Can I check? On the right of the snacks?

B: Yes. Opposite the fruit.

A: Thank you.

B: You're welcome.

Conversation 3

A: Excuse me, where are the cakes?

B: I think they're near the snacks.

A: Near the snacks. Which way?

B: I'm not sure. I know the cereal is opposite the snacks …

A: Cereal? What's that?

B: Cereal. Like Corn Flakes.

A: Er … ?

B: Erm, for breakfast. You have it with milk.

A: Oh, OK.

B: Yes, so the cereal is opposite the snacks.

A: OK, and the cakes?

B: I think they're on the right of the cereal.

A: On the right. Thank you.

B: No problem. Or maybe …

A: Thank you!

UNIT 8 Recording 6

This is my bad holiday story. Last year I went to Hawaii on holiday. First, I missed my plane,

so I took another plane. I arrived in Honolulu one day late. The weather was very bad, and it rained for the first three days. I stayed in my hotel room and read a book. The hotel was noisy because my room was next to the road. There was a restaurant, but the food was expensive, and it wasn't very good. I was there for two weeks, and I was very happy to go home.

REVIEW 4 Recording 1

1 My name's Sara. I'm the receptionist in the hotel. Mr Black and Mr Brown went out yesterday afternoon at a quarter to two. They came back together … at about half past three, and they went to their rooms.

2 My name's Alan. I'm a waiter in the hotel restaurant. I was in the restaurant last night. There were two men and a woman in the restaurant all evening. One man and the woman danced for about half an hour – from half past nine to ten o'clock. They all left at ten o'clock.

3 I'm a guest in the hotel. My room is on the right of Mr and Mrs Black's room. Their radio was on last night from about ten to eleven. It was very noisy!

4 I'm the night receptionist. Mr Black went out at ten o'clock. He said he wanted to take a walk. Then at a quarter past ten, another man went out. I didn't see him very well. Maybe it was Mr Brown. I don't know.

5 My name's Mary White. I'm a guest in the hotel. I came back from the town at about half past ten. I saw a woman in front of the hotel. She had men's clothes: a man's jacket, a man's trousers and a man's hat. I was surprised, you know. A woman in a man's clothes. Was there a party or something?

UNIT 9 Recording 3

1 A shopping mistake? Um … well my boyfriend wanted to go camping, so I bought him a tent. It was a good tent. I paid seventy pounds for it. Anyway, he put it up in the garden – once, I think. Imagine that, just one time! He never used it again. It was a waste of money. The truth is he really likes hotels!

2 I don't really know … Oh yeah, last year my wife bought me an exercise bike. I thought it was a good idea, too, but you know, I think I used it three times. It was hard work! A real waste of money!

3 Shopping mistakes? Oh, that's easy. Clothes. I often buy clothes and then when I get them home I don't like them. For example, last month I went shopping with a friend and I bought a hat. It cost a hundred euros. My friend said it looked beautiful. My boyfriend said it was terrible … so I sold it … on the internet. I got fifty euros for it. It was a real waste of money.

4 A shopping mistake? Oh yes, all the time. For example, I got my sister's little boy some drums, for his birthday. I thought it was a good idea. He loves those drums. He plays them all day. So he's happy … but my sister isn't happy. Now she doesn't talk to me! I phoned her yesterday, but she didn't answer.

5 A shopping mistake. Erm … oh yeah, my mother gave us a lamp. We didn't like it, but I know it cost her a lot of money. Then after a week I broke it. I tried to fix it but it was impossible. Whoops!

UNIT 9 Recording 6

A: Hi, Tom. It's Lisa.

B: Oh hi, Lisa. How are you?

A: Fine thanks. Listen, what would you like for your birthday?

B: Oh, I don't know. Let me think … I don't know.

A: I'm in Bridge's Department Store, so it's a good time to tell me …

B: Um … well, maybe something from the World Cup.

A: For example?

B: Er …

A: Well, would you like a football shirt, or … ?

B: Um … no. Oh, I know! I'd like a DVD.

A: Of the World Cup?

B: Yeah.

A: OK.

B: Great, thanks.

A: No problem. Bye.

B: Bye.

A: Excuse me, can you help me? Where's the Sports department?

C: It's over there. Behind the Toys department.

A: Thanks.

D: Can I help you?

A: Yes, I'd like a DVD of the World Cup, but there aren't any DVDs here.

D: No, the sports DVDs are in Home Entertainment. In the DVD section.

A: Where's that?

D: It's opposite Computers and Phones. Over there.

A: Thanks.

Yeah, I'd like a DVD of the World Cup, but there are two different DVDs here. Which DVD is best, do you think?

E: Er … let me see … this one has all the important matches.

A: How much is it? Ah, I see. Twenty euros. OK, can I have this?

C: Yes, you pay over there.

A: Oh, right. Thanks.

E: No problem.

UNIT 9 Recording 9

1 What's your favourite fruit?

2 Where were you last Saturday afternoon?

3 Do you want a new car?

4 What did you study in the last lesson?

UNIT 9 Recording 10

One of my favourite possessions is my camera. It's very small, and I keep it in my bag. I bought it last year in New York. I like it because it's easy to use and it takes very good photos. I take photos of my friends, and of places and of me. I have a lot of photos of me in different places. I put them on my website. I travel a lot, and I usually travel alone, but my camera is my travel partner.

UNIT 10 Recording 1

Conversation 1

A: So, Greg. Thanks for coming in.

B: No problem.

A: Right, I have some questions for you.

B: OK.

AUDIO SCRIPTS

A: Er … first of all, can you ride a motorbike?
B: Yes, um … yes, I can. Of course.
A: That's good. And do you know the city well? Can you find a place, fast?
B: Yes, I can. No problem.
A: And in this job you sometimes work alone …
B: That's not a problem.
A: … but you meet a lot of people.
B: I like people.
A: OK, good. Oh, and we sometimes get very busy and we need help in the kitchen – cleaning or cooking. Is that OK?
B: Yeah, no problem. I worked in a café last year and I made sandwiches … and pizzas.
A: Great! Can you start tomorrow?
B: Sure. Wow, I got the job?
A: Yes, congratulations! Come and look at the motorbike.
B: Oh, it's big.
A: Yeah, here you go. Try it.
B: Oh, er, OK. It's a bit difficult to ride. But I'm sure I can learn.
A: Be careful!
B: Aaah!
A: Oh, no! Greg, are you OK? Next interview, I think.

Conversation 2

A: So, you think this is the job for you.
B: Yeah, yeah I do.
A: OK, can you sing?
B: Yeah, I can. And I can play guitar.
C: OK, great. Let's hear something.
B: All right, here we go.
C: Not bad! … OK, that's good. Nice. And what about dancing?
B: Ah … I can dance, but not very well.
A: Mmm. OK, but you can sing well and you're good on guitar.
C: OK, we'd like to try you … for a month.
B: That's great!

Conversation 3

A: So, what languages can you speak?
B: English, Japanese, Russian.
A: Great. And can you drive?
B: Yes.
A: OK. And can you remember facts and information?
B: Yes, I can. I have a very good memory.
A: So, can you remember my name?
B: Er … Did you say your name? Erm … Sorry, I can't remember.
A: Oh, dear … OK, let's try some other questions.

UNIT 10   Recording 3

1 Can you sing?
2 Yes, I can.
3 I can play guitar too.
4 Can you dance?
5 No, I can't.
6 I can't dance.

UNIT 10   Recording 4

Conversation 1

A: Hi, do you have a minute?
B: Yeah, sure.
A: What's your name?
B: Tom.

A: OK, Tom. Can you look at this list? It's people's top ten goals in life.
B: Oh, OK.
A: So, do you have a goal for this year?
B: A goal? Yes, I want to learn something new. My girlfriend can cook really well, but she doesn't like cooking. So I'm going to learn to cook.
A: That's interesting. Any special type of cooking?
B: Yeah, Japanese food. I lived in Japan and I love Japanese food.
A: I see, well …

Conversation 2

A: So, Fiona, do you have a goal for this year?
C: I'm going to change jobs.
A: That's a big change!
C: Yeah, well, I work in an office, and I don't like it. I'd like to work outside.
A: Great.
C: My friend Sheila is going to help me.
A: Well, good luck with that.
C: Thanks!

Conversation 3

A: Liam, do you have a goal for this year?
D: Yes, I do.
A: So, what are you going to do?
D: Well, I work with computers, sometimes twelve hours a day and I often take work home. It isn't good …
A: Right.
D: … so this year I'm going to spend more time with my friends and I'm not going to take work home.
A: Great.

Conversation 4

A: Rudi, what are your goals?
E: Er … I'm going to get fit. I never do sport. I can't play tennis or anything, but I'm going to start exercising. Something easy. Take a walk every day.
A: Sounds good.

Conversation 5

A: What's your goal this year, Alex?
F: I have two goals really.
A: Oh, and what are they?
F: One is to save more money. The other is to see my friends more.
A: That's great. And what are your plans? With your friends?
F: Well … hmm … maybe go shopping together.
A: Go shopping? Then you aren't going to save money!
F: Yeah, but I'm not going to stop shopping!

UNIT 10   Recording 6

Conversation 1

A: Hi, Duncan.
B: Hi, how are you?
A: Good thanks. Hey, this is a great place.
B: Yes, it's really good. I often come here.
A: … well, that was delicious. Let's have coffee.
B: OK … wait, is that the time? I'm sorry, I have a lesson at two. Here's some money for lunch.
A: No, that's all right. Keep in touch!
B: See you in two weeks, after the holidays, yeah?
A: Oh yes, that's right. See you then …

Conversation 2

A: Excuse me, do you have the time?
B: Yes, it's half past four.
A: Thanks. So … erm … where are you going?
B: Me? I'm going to … so you're from Madrid. That's interesting.
A: Yes, well, I come from Córdoba. I moved to Madrid when I was ten.
B: I see … oh, look, this is my station.
A: Look, here's my card.
B: And here's mine.
A: Very nice to meet you.
B: Nice to meet you, too.
A: I hope we meet again.
B: I hope so, too.
A: Goodbye.
B: Bye!

Conversation 3

A: What do you think of the music?
B: It's not bad.
A: Hi, I'm Doug.
B: Oh, hello. I'm Jo.
A: So, are you from around here?
B: No, I'm not actually. I'm from …
A: … yes and I was in China the next year. I speak Chinese, you know.
B: Oh, really?
A: And I speak four other languages. French, German, Spanish …
B: I'm sorry, I can see an old friend over there. Nice to talk to you.
A: Oh … and you.
B: See you later.
A: See you soon.

UNIT 10   Recording 9

Three years ago I bought a guitar. I wanted to learn to play guitar because I can sing and I like music. I tried to learn it alone. I had a book and I practised every day. I learned some songs, and I played guitar and sang the songs. I was happy, but then my boyfriend said I wasn't very good at it. He said I needed a teacher. So I found a teacher, and studied guitar with him. The teacher was great but it was very different because he gave me homework every week. After four months I played guitar really well. I still play every day.

REVIEW 5   Recording 1

1 I want to learn a lot of vocabulary, so I'm going to learn seven new words every day. I like reading, so I'm going to look at the BBC news website and write down new words.
2 Speaking is a problem for me. In the coffee break, I'm not going to speak in my language. I'm going to speak in English. All the time!
3 I can't understand English very well, so I'm going to practise listening. I'm going to listen to my CD and read the audio scripts at the same time.
4 My grammar is bad. Very bad! I'm going to look on the internet and do some extra grammar practice.
5 I want to improve my writing, so I'm going to write a diary every night, in English. I'm going to write about my day.